Test Taking: Grade
Table of Contents

Introduction to STARS 2	
Letter to Parents............................4	
DOs and DON'Ts 5	
Practice Test Answer Sheet..........6	

UNIT I: WORD ANALYSIS
- Lesson 1: Structural Analysis of Words 7
- Lesson 2: Word Classification 9
- Lesson 3: Prefixes, Suffixes, and Root Words 10
- Lesson 4: Compound Words 12
- Practice Test 1 13

UNIT II: VOCABULARY
- Lesson 1: Discovering Analogies 16
- Lesson 2: Thinking about Word Origins 18
- Lesson 3: Thinking about Word Relationships 19
- Lesson 4: Homographs—Words with More Than One Meaning 21
- Lesson 5: Using Context Clues 22
- Practice Test 2 24

UNIT III: GRAMMAR PRACTICE
- Lesson 1: Identifying Nouns, Verbs, and Pronouns 28
- Lesson 2: Identifying Adjectives and Adverbs 29
- Lesson 3: Identifying Conjunctions and Prepositions 30
- Lesson 4: Identifying Simple, Compound, and Complex Sentences 31
- Practice Test 3 32

UNIT IV: LANGUAGE USAGE
- Lesson 1: Identifying Correct Spelling 35
- Lesson 2: Identifying Correct Capitalization and Punctuation 36
- Lesson 3: Proofreading Compositions 37
- Lesson 4: Identifying Complete Subjects and Predicates 39
- Lesson 5: Practicing with Pronouns 40
- Lesson 6: Using Degrees of Comparison 42
- Lesson 7: Identifying Interjections 44
- Practice Test 4 45

UNIT V:
- Lesson 1: Outlining 50
- Lesson 2: Understanding Visual Information.............................52
- Lesson 3: Using an Index 54
- Lesson 4: Using a Table of Contents 55
- Lesson 5: Using Dictionary Skills 56
- Practice Test 5 58

UNIT VI: READING COMPREHENSION
- Lesson 1: Finding the Main Idea 62
- Lesson 2: Drawing Conclusions..................64
- Lesson 3: Recognizing Cause and Effect...66
- Lesson 4: Recognizing Fact and Opinion 68
- Practice Test 6 70

UNIT VII: MATH CONCEPTS AND COMPUTATION
- Lesson 1: Understanding Numeration and Practicing Computation 74
- Lesson 2: Understanding Number Theory and Using Estimation 76
- Lesson 3: Working with Fractions 77
- Lesson 4: Working with Decimals 78
- Lesson 5: Working with Ratio, Percent, and Probability 79
- Lesson 6: Understanding Geometry and Measurement..........................80
- Lesson 7: Using Graphs and Tables............82
- Practice Test 7 83

UNIT VIII: PROBLEM SOLVING
- Lesson 1: Understanding Problem Solving Strategies 86
- Lesson 2: Practicing Problem Solving..........88
- Practice Test 8 91

Answer Key...95

© Steck-Vaughn Company

Test Taking 6, SV 6774-3

TEST TAKING STARS
(Strategies To Achieve Raised Scores)

INTRODUCTION

Test Taking is a tool to assist your students in learning to take tests. Research shows that students who are acquainted with the scoring format of standardized tests score higher on these tests. Students also score higher when they practice and encounter the pressures of timed tests. The concepts presented for practice are typically found on standardized tests for students at the sixth-grade level. *The scores on these activities are indicators of a student's ability to take tests, not necessarily to master the concepts used for practice.* Students who practice with STARS will grow comfortable with the variety of processes needed to improve test scores.

ORGANIZATION

Each of the eight units focuses on specific test taking areas in content: Word Analysis, Vocabulary, Grammar Practice, Language Usage, Study Skills, Reading Comprehension, Math Concepts and Computation, and Problem Solving. Practice lessons introduce students to the typical formats they can expect to see. These pages identify strategy tips for improving accuracy and speed. At the bottom of each lesson, students are encouraged to evaluate their performance. Again, the goal is to improve students' ability to perform well on tests. At the end of each unit, a practice test is included. Students have the opportunity to apply the strategies they learned in the lessons and to demonstrate their abilities to successfully complete a test.

USE

STARS is designed for independent use by students who have had instruction in the specific skills covered in these workbooks. Copies of the activities can be given to individuals, pairs of students, or small groups for completion. They can also be used as a center activity.

To begin, determine the implementation which fits your students' needs and your classroom structure. The following plan suggests a format for this implementation:

1. Explain the purpose of the worksheets to your class.

2. Review the mechanics of how you want students to work with the exercises. Do you want to check the practice lessons before they begin the practice tests? Do you want to discuss the samples in each lesson?

3. Determine how the timed tests will be monitored. If students are to do the timed tests on their own, what timing instrument should they use? Do you want to administer the timed tests to the whole class or to a group that has successfully completed a series of practice lessons?

4. Introduce students to the process and to the purpose of the activities. Make copies of the **DOs and DON'Ts** for test taking, and review with students.

5. Assure students that all of the material is for practice purposes only. It is to help them do better on tests.

6. Do a practice activity together.

ADDITIONAL NOTES

1. Time Limits. The time limits for each practice test are suggested limits. You may choose to ignore them or to set limits which you think are more appropriate for your students.

2. Parent Communication. Sign the **Letter to Parents**. Duplicate and send home with the students. Decide if you want to keep the activity pages and practice tests in portfolios for conferencing, or if you want students to take them home as they complete them.

3. Bulletin Board. Display the **DOs and DON'Ts** for test taking in your classroom for quick reference.

4. Student Evaluation. In the student evaluation section of the practice activities, encourage students to identify interferences that affect their performance on tests, such as conflicts with peers, lack of sleep, inadequate breakfast, etc.

5. Have fun. Reducing the pressure associated with test taking can be fun as well as meaningful for you and your students. Look forward to positive results and to improved test scores!

Dear Parent,

Sometime during this school year, our class will be taking mandated standardized tests. To increase your child's skills in test taking, we will be working with sample tests to give him or her the tools to perform well. Test taking can be stressful. By working together to prepare the students, we can reduce their stress level.

From time to time, I may send home lesson practice sheets. To best help your child, please consider the following suggestions:

- Provide a quiet place to work.
- Go over the directions and the sample exercises together.
- Review the Strategy Tips.
- Reassure your child that the practice sheets are not a "real" test.
- Encourage your child to do his or her best.
- Record the amount of time it takes to complete the lesson.
- Check the lesson when it is complete.
- Go over the answers and note improvements as well as problems.

Help your child maintain a positive attitude about taking a standardized test. Let your child know that each test provides an opportunity to shine. If your child expresses anxiety about taking a test or completing these lessons, help him or her understand what causes the stress. Then, talk about ways to eliminate anxiety. Above all, enjoy this time you spend with your child. He or she will feel your support, and test scores will improve as success in test taking is experienced.

Thank you for your help!

Cordially,

Name_____   Date _____

STARS DOs AND DON'Ts FOR TEST TAKING

DO:
- listen to or read all the directions.
- read all the samples and STRATEGY TIPS for each lesson before you begin.
- look over the entire test or section before you begin.
- stay calm, concentrate on the test, and clear your mind of things that have nothing to do with the test.
- read all the answer choices before choosing the one that you think is best.
- make sure the number you fill in on the answer sheet matches the question number on the test page.
- trust your first instinct when answering each question.
- answer the easy questions first, then go back and work on the ones you aren't sure about.
- take all the time you are allowed.

DON'T:
- look ahead to another question until you complete the one you're working on.
- spend too much time on one question.
- rush.
- worry if others finish while you are still working.
- change an answer unless you are really sure it should be changed.

DO your very best!

Name_____   Date _____

Practice Test ____ Answer Sheet

1. Ⓐ Ⓑ Ⓒ Ⓓ Ⓔ   21. Ⓐ Ⓑ Ⓒ Ⓓ Ⓔ
2. Ⓐ Ⓑ Ⓒ Ⓓ Ⓔ   22. Ⓐ Ⓑ Ⓒ Ⓓ Ⓔ
3. Ⓐ Ⓑ Ⓒ Ⓓ Ⓔ   23. Ⓐ Ⓑ Ⓒ Ⓓ Ⓔ
4. Ⓐ Ⓑ Ⓒ Ⓓ Ⓔ   24. Ⓐ Ⓑ Ⓒ Ⓓ Ⓔ
5. Ⓐ Ⓑ Ⓒ Ⓓ Ⓔ   25. Ⓐ Ⓑ Ⓒ Ⓓ Ⓔ
6. Ⓐ Ⓑ Ⓒ Ⓓ Ⓔ   26. Ⓐ Ⓑ Ⓒ Ⓓ Ⓔ
7. Ⓐ Ⓑ Ⓒ Ⓓ Ⓔ   27. Ⓐ Ⓑ Ⓒ Ⓓ Ⓔ
8. Ⓐ Ⓑ Ⓒ Ⓓ Ⓔ   28. Ⓐ Ⓑ Ⓒ Ⓓ Ⓔ
9. Ⓐ Ⓑ Ⓒ Ⓓ Ⓔ   29. Ⓐ Ⓑ Ⓒ Ⓓ Ⓔ
10. Ⓐ Ⓑ Ⓒ Ⓓ Ⓔ   30. Ⓐ Ⓑ Ⓒ Ⓓ Ⓔ
11. Ⓐ Ⓑ Ⓒ Ⓓ Ⓔ   31. Ⓐ Ⓑ Ⓒ Ⓓ Ⓔ
12. Ⓐ Ⓑ Ⓒ Ⓓ Ⓔ   32. Ⓐ Ⓑ Ⓒ Ⓓ Ⓔ
13. Ⓐ Ⓑ Ⓒ Ⓓ Ⓔ   33. Ⓐ Ⓑ Ⓒ Ⓓ Ⓔ
14. Ⓐ Ⓑ Ⓒ Ⓓ Ⓔ   34. Ⓐ Ⓑ Ⓒ Ⓓ Ⓔ
15. Ⓐ Ⓑ Ⓒ Ⓓ Ⓔ   35. Ⓐ Ⓑ Ⓒ Ⓓ Ⓔ
16. Ⓐ Ⓑ Ⓒ Ⓓ Ⓔ   36. Ⓐ Ⓑ Ⓒ Ⓓ Ⓔ
17. Ⓐ Ⓑ Ⓒ Ⓓ Ⓔ   37. Ⓐ Ⓑ Ⓒ Ⓓ Ⓔ
18. Ⓐ Ⓑ Ⓒ Ⓓ Ⓔ   38. Ⓐ Ⓑ Ⓒ Ⓓ Ⓔ
19. Ⓐ Ⓑ Ⓒ Ⓓ Ⓔ   39. Ⓐ Ⓑ Ⓒ Ⓓ Ⓔ
20. Ⓐ Ⓑ Ⓒ Ⓓ Ⓔ   40. Ⓐ Ⓑ Ⓒ Ⓓ Ⓔ

© Steck-Vaughn Company   Test Taking 6, SV 6774-3

Name_____ Date _____

UNIT I: WORD ANALYSIS

Lesson 1: Structural analysis of words
Part one

DIRECTIONS ▶ Darken the circle for the number that tells how many syllables are in each of the following words.

1. Remember that every syllable must have at least one vowel sound.
2. Syllables are usually divided between consonants.

Sample:
How many syllables does the word <u>exclamation</u> have?

Ⓐ 3   Ⓒ 5
Ⓑ 2   Ⓓ 4

ANSWER

The correct answer is *D 4*. There are 4 syllables in ex.cla.ma.tion.

NOW TRY THESE

1. How many syllables does the word <u>disrupted</u> have?
   Ⓐ 2   Ⓒ 3
   Ⓑ 4   Ⓓ 1

2. How many syllables are there in <u>collapse</u>?
   Ⓐ 3   Ⓒ 4
   Ⓑ 2   Ⓓ 5

3. How many syllables are there in <u>exaggeration</u>?
   Ⓐ 3   Ⓒ 4
   Ⓑ 2   Ⓓ 5

4. How many syllables does the word <u>untimely</u> have?
   Ⓐ 2   Ⓒ 4
   Ⓑ 3   Ⓓ 5

5. How many syllables are there in <u>tardiness</u>?
   Ⓐ 5   Ⓒ 3
   Ⓑ 4   Ⓓ 2

Name_____   Date _____

Part two

DIRECTIONS ▶ Darken the circle for the word that stands for a contraction, a possessive noun, or the plural form of a noun.

 **STRATEGY TIPS**

1. A contraction has an apostrophe to show that one or more letters have been left out.
2. The possessive form of singular nouns is usually shown by adding an apostrophe and an **s**. The possessive form of plural nouns ending in **s** is usually shown by adding an apostrophe at the end.
3. Remember the exceptions to adding **s** when you form plural nouns.

Sample:
Which of the following words is a contraction?

- Ⓐ kid's
- Ⓑ friends'
- Ⓒ sister's
- Ⓓ wouldn't

 **ANSWER**

The correct answer is *D wouldn't*. The other words show possessives.

NOW TRY THESE

6. Which of the following words is a contraction?
   - Ⓐ let's
   - Ⓑ needle's
   - Ⓒ newspaper's
   - Ⓓ teacher's

7. Which of these words is a possessive noun?
   - Ⓐ wife's
   - Ⓑ stores
   - Ⓒ wives
   - Ⓓ there's

8. Which of these words is a contraction?
   - Ⓐ your
   - Ⓑ children's
   - Ⓒ it's
   - Ⓓ sister's

9. Which word is the correct plural form of a noun?
   - Ⓐ loafs
   - Ⓑ rodeos
   - Ⓒ soloes
   - Ⓓ skys

Part three

DIRECTIONS ▶ Darken the circle for the contraction that best completes the sentence.

10. _____ a long journey down to the bottom of the mountain.
    - Ⓐ We're
    - Ⓑ She's
    - Ⓒ They'll
    - Ⓓ We've

11. Joan said that _____ cook dinner for us.
    - Ⓐ they're
    - Ⓑ I'm
    - Ⓒ she'd
    - Ⓓ he's

STOP

Your time:_____

Number right:_____

Name_____   Date _____

Lesson 2: Word classification

DIRECTIONS ▶ Darken the circle for the word that best fits with the other words in the group.

STRATEGY TIP

Think about the way in which each group of words is connected. What do they have in common?

Sample:
Which word would go with **tea, beef, pasta, cream**?

Ⓐ refrigerator   Ⓒ history
Ⓑ artichoke   Ⓓ oven

ANSWER

The correct answer is *B artichoke*. The words in the group are foods. An *artichoke* is a kind of food.

NOW TRY THESE

1. armoire, rocker, table, shelf
   Ⓐ hammer   Ⓒ tapioca
   Ⓑ blue   Ⓓ bed

2. teacher, typist, ranger, medic
   Ⓐ team   Ⓒ electric
   Ⓑ engineer Ⓓ salmon

3. drill, tire iron, wrench, pliers
   Ⓐ car   Ⓒ home
   Ⓑ boat   Ⓓ ruler

4. watermelon, peach, orange, tangerine
   Ⓐ rice   Ⓒ bread
   Ⓑ kiwi   Ⓓ fish

5. wind surfing, in-line skating, canoeing, sailing
   Ⓐ waking   Ⓒ talking
   Ⓑ singing Ⓓ kayaking

6. football, wrestling, swimming, baseball
   Ⓐ karate   Ⓒ cooking
   Ⓑ sewing   Ⓓ stadium

7. opera, play, program, drama
   Ⓐ magician Ⓒ team
   Ⓑ concert Ⓓ class

8. pleased, happy, angry, furious
   Ⓐ delighted Ⓒ lazy
   Ⓑ hungry   Ⓓ neat

9. squirrel, rabbit, kangaroo, wildcat,
   Ⓐ farm   Ⓒ buffalo
   Ⓑ woods   Ⓓ barn

10. beech, oak, elm, birch
    Ⓐ fruit   Ⓒ sycamore
    Ⓑ vegetable Ⓓ friend

Your time:_____
Number right:_____

Lesson 3: Prefixes, suffixes, and root words
Part one

DIRECTIONS ▶ Darken the circle for the root word that has a prefix, suffix, or both added to it.

STRATEGY TIP

Remember that a root word is a word that can be combined with prefixes and suffixes to make a new word.

Sample:

Which is the root word of <u>repacked</u>?

- Ⓐ repack
- Ⓑ pack
- Ⓒ packed
- Ⓓ acked

ANSWER

The correct answer is *B pack*. The word *pack* has both a prefix and a suffix added to it.

NOW TRY THESE

1. Which is the root word of <u>telegraph</u>?
   - Ⓐ graph
   - Ⓑ tele
   - Ⓒ tel
   - Ⓓ rap

2. Which is the root word of <u>delightful</u>?
   - Ⓐ light
   - Ⓑ ful
   - Ⓒ delight
   - Ⓓ deli

3. Which is the root word of <u>bacteriology</u>?
   - Ⓐ bacteria
   - Ⓑ ology
   - Ⓒ logy
   - Ⓓ bacter

4. Which is the root word of <u>inexcusable</u>?
   - Ⓐ in
   - Ⓑ able
   - Ⓒ usable
   - Ⓓ excuse

5. Which is the root word of <u>dislocated</u>?
   - Ⓐ located
   - Ⓑ locate
   - Ⓒ dislocate
   - Ⓓ local

GO ON TO NEXT PAGE ▶

Name_____   Date _____

Part two

DIRECTIONS ▶ Darken the circle for the affix (either prefix or suffix) that has been added to a root word.

Sample:
Which affix makes multimillion mean *many millions*?

Ⓐ million   Ⓒ mill
Ⓑ multi   Ⓓ lion

ANSWER
The correct answer is *B multi*.
The prefix *multi* means *many*.

NOW TRY THESE

6. Which affix makes astrology mean *the study of stars*?

   Ⓐ ology   Ⓒ astrol
   Ⓑ astro   Ⓓ ast

7. Which affix makes autobiography mean *the story of a person's life written by that person*?

   Ⓐ graph   Ⓒ auto
   Ⓑ bio   Ⓓ graphy

8. Which affix makes thermometer mean *an instrument to measure heat*?

   Ⓐ meter   Ⓒ therm
   Ⓑ the   Ⓓ er

9. Which affix makes portable mean *able to be carried*?

   Ⓐ port   Ⓒ por
   Ⓑ able   Ⓓ le

Part three

DIRECTIONS ▶ Darken the letter for the affix that makes a word to fit the definition.

Sample:
Which affix added to state makes a word that means *between states*?

Ⓐ bi   Ⓒ ful
Ⓑ dis   Ⓓ inter

ANSWER
The correct answer is *D inter*.
The prefix *inter* means *between*.

NOW TRY THESE

10. Which affix added to spell makes a word that means *badly spelled*?

    Ⓐ bi   Ⓒ un
    Ⓑ mis   Ⓓ ed

11. Which affix added to hero makes a word that means *like a hero*?

    Ⓐ ly   Ⓒ ish
    Ⓑ ful   Ⓓ ic

Your time:_____
Number right:_____

Name_____   Date_____

Lesson 4: Compound words

DIRECTIONS ▶ Darken the circle for the compound word that matches the definition.

STRATEGY TIPS
1. Think about the three kinds of compound words before you answer.
2. Closed compounds are two words written together as one. (eyebrow)
3. Open compounds are words used together but written separately. (fire engine)
4. Hyphenated compounds are words joined by hyphens. (know-how)

Sample:
Letters carried by plane.

Ⓐ airplane   Ⓒ air time
Ⓑ airmail   Ⓓ air space

ANSWER
The correct answer is *B airmail.*

NOW TRY THESE

1. A special building for children.
   Ⓐ playground   Ⓒ playhouse
   Ⓑ play-off   Ⓓ play land

2. Your relationship to your father's grandfather.
   Ⓐ grandson   Ⓒ grandchild
   Ⓑ great-grandchild   Ⓓ granddaughter

3. Not completely cooked.
   Ⓐ half-baked   Ⓒ half time
   Ⓑ unbaked   Ⓓ sunbaked

4. A signal used to control traffic.
   Ⓐ stopwatch   Ⓒ stoplight
   Ⓑ flashlight   Ⓓ stop street

5. Someone who saves people from drowning.
   Ⓐ lifetime   Ⓒ life raft
   Ⓑ life net   Ⓓ lifeguard

6. A kind of spread used in sandwiches.
   Ⓐ butternut   Ⓒ peanut butter
   Ⓑ butterfly   Ⓓ buttercup

7. The center of a target.
   Ⓐ eyeball   Ⓒ eyelash
   Ⓑ bull's-eye Ⓓ bulldog

8. A game played in a swimming pool.
   Ⓐ water front   Ⓒ water polo
   Ⓑ waterfall   Ⓓ water power

STOP

Your time:_____

Number right:_____

Name_____ Date _____

PRACTICE TEST 1

Part 1

Directions: For questions 1-4, darken the circle on the answer sheet for the number that tells how many syllables are in each of the following words.

Sample: gigantic
- A 2
- B 4
- C 3
- D 5

Answer: The correct answer is *C 3*.

---

1. irreplaceable
   - A 4
   - B 5
   - C 6
   - D 3

2. interrupt
   - A 3
   - B 4
   - C 2
   - D 5

3. seventh
   - A 3
   - B 2
   - C 4
   - D 1

4. vacation
   - A 4
   - B 2
   - C 3
   - D 5

Part 2

Directions: For questions 5-6, darken the circle on the answer sheet for the word that stands for a contraction, a possessive noun, or the plural form of a noun.

Sample: Which of the following words is the possessive form of a noun?
- A we're
- B dog's
- C kittens
- D ours

Answer: The correct answer is *B dog's*.

---

5. Which of these is the plural form of a noun?
   - A children's
   - B owner's
   - C bushes
   - D foot

6. Which of these words is a contraction?
   - A it's
   - B book's
   - C horse's
   - D teacher's

Name_____ Date _____

Test One: Word Analysis

Part 3

Directions: For questions 7-10, darken the circle on the answer sheet for the word that best fits with the other words in each group.

Sample: thimble, scissors, pattern, needle

    A paper   **C** fabric
    B table   **D** book

Answer: The correct answer is *C fabric*.

---

7. rain, sleet, snow, hurricane

    A storm   **C** beach
    B game   **D** sun

8. judge, court, lawyer, jury

    A school   **C** witness
    B room   **D** building

9. grocery, bakery, dairy, delicatessen

    A supermarket   **C** hotel
    B camp   **D** nursery

10. books, magazines, newspapers, letters

    A paper   **C** pamphlets
    B ink   **D** chapters

Part 4

Directions: For questions 11-14, darken the circle on the answer sheet for the letter of the root word that has had a prefix or suffix added to it.

Sample: Which is the root word of <u>refinished</u>?

    A refine   **C** shed
    B fin   **D** finish

Answer: The correct answer is *D finish*.

---

11. Which is the root word of <u>frightfully</u>?

    A fully   **C** full
    B fright   **D** frightful

12. Which is the root word of <u>spectacular</u>?

    A tacular   **C** spectacle
    B spect   **D** lar

13. Which is the root word of <u>discussion</u>?

    A discuss   **C** dis
    B cuss   **D** cussion

14. Which is the root word of <u>mistaken</u>?

    A taken   **C** mistake
    B take   **D** stake

GO ON TO NEXT PAGE

Name_____ Date_____

Part 5

Directions: For questions 15-19, darken the circle on the answer sheet for the letter of the affix that has been added to the underlined word.

Sample: Which affix makes furious mean *full of anger*?

  A fur   C fury
  B ous   D us

Answer: The correct answer is *B ous*.

---

15. Which affix makes invaluable mean *priceless*?

    A value   C valuable
    B able   D in

16. Which affix makes misleading mean *deceptive*?

    A mis   C leading
    B lead D ing

17. Which affix makes collection mean *a group of things*?

    A collect   C tion
    B lect   D col

18. Which affix makes combustible mean *apt to catch fire*?

    A com   C le
    B ible   D bust

19. Which affix makes recognize mean *to know again*?

    A re   C recon
    B ize   D cog

Suggested Time Limit: 22 minutes   Your time: _____
Check your work if you have time. Wait for instructions from your teacher.

Name_____ Date _____

UNIT II: VOCABULARY

Lesson 1: Discovering analogies

DIRECTIONS ▸ Darken the circle for the word that completes the analogy (how the ideas are connected). Darken the circle for *E none* if the correct answer is not given.

STRATEGY TIPS

1. Remember, analogies explain ideas by comparing them to ideas that are familiar to the reader.
2. Decide how the ideas in the first pair of words are connected.
3. Read the question word. Find another word that is connected to it the same way that the first pair of words is connected.

Sample:

red : apple = yellow : _____

- Ⓐ book
- Ⓑ game
- Ⓒ sun
- Ⓓ fruit
- Ⓔ none

ANSWER

The correct answer is *C sun*. The color yellow is usually used to show the sun.

NOW TRY THESE

1. students : school = athletes : _____
    - Ⓐ team
    - Ⓑ room
    - Ⓒ home
    - Ⓓ street
    - Ⓔ none

2. broad : width = tall : _____
    - Ⓐ long
    - Ⓑ short
    - Ⓒ height
    - Ⓓ weight
    - Ⓔ none

3. blades : ice skates = wheels : _____
    - Ⓐ surf boards
    - Ⓑ roller skates
    - Ⓒ knives
    - Ⓓ scissors
    - Ⓔ none

4. teach : reach = mind : _____
    - Ⓐ think
    - Ⓑ listen
    - Ⓒ head
    - Ⓓ care
    - Ⓔ none

5. mend : repair = break : _____
    - Ⓐ burn
    - Ⓑ destroy
    - Ⓒ cut
    - Ⓓ tear
    - Ⓔ none

6. forward : backward = approach : _____
    - Ⓐ avoid
    - Ⓑ near
    - Ⓒ enter
    - Ⓓ touch
    - Ⓔ none

7. football : field = basketball : _____
    - Ⓐ diamond
    - Ⓑ court
    - Ⓒ table
    - Ⓓ goal
    - Ⓔ none

8. pool : swim = library : _____
    - Ⓐ paper
    - Ⓑ read
    - Ⓒ building
    - Ⓓ splash
    - Ⓔ none

GO ON TO NEXT PAGE

Name_____   Date _____

Unit II, lesson 1, page 2

9. November : Thanksgiving = March : _____
   - Ⓐ St. Patrick's Day
   - Ⓑ Labor Day
   - Ⓒ Election Day
   - Ⓓ Memorial Day
   - Ⓔ none

10. purple : plum = black : _____
    - Ⓐ apple
    - Ⓑ tree
    - Ⓒ coal
    - Ⓓ white
    - Ⓔ none

11. lamp : light = furnace : _____
    - Ⓐ heat
    - Ⓑ dark
    - Ⓒ cold
    - Ⓓ house
    - Ⓔ none

12. last : lose = first : _____
    - Ⓐ run
    - Ⓑ play
    - Ⓒ relay
    - Ⓓ win
    - Ⓔ none

13. clear : clever = class : _____
    - Ⓐ clap
    - Ⓑ dull
    - Ⓒ room
    - Ⓓ camp
    - Ⓔ none

14. bread : head = meat : _____
    - Ⓐ feat
    - Ⓑ chop
    - Ⓒ milk
    - Ⓓ cheese
    - Ⓔ none

15. violin : orchestra = checker : _____
    - Ⓐ band
    - Ⓑ game
    - Ⓒ token
    - Ⓓ red
    - Ⓔ none

16. movie : film = book : _____
    - Ⓐ camera
    - Ⓑ chapter
    - Ⓒ paper
    - Ⓓ shelf
    - Ⓔ none

Your time: _____
Number right: _____

On this lesson I did _____ because _____
_____.

I think it would help me to _____
_____
_____.

Name_____   Date _____

Lesson 2: Thinking about word origins

DIRECTIONS ▶ Darken the circle for the word that comes from another language. Darken the circle for *E none* if the correct answer is <u>not given</u>.

 **STRATEGY TIPS**

1. Read the meaning of the foreign word.
2. Choose the word that is closest in sound and meaning to the original word.

Sample:
Which word comes from the Spanish <u>batata</u> meaning a *kind of vegetable*?

Ⓐ bath   Ⓒ carrot   Ⓔ none
Ⓑ potato Ⓓ beet

ANSWER
The correct answer is *B potato*. A potato is a vegetable. The word *potato* sounds similar to *batata*.

 **NOW TRY THESE**

1. Which word comes from the Spanish <u>hamaca</u>, meaning *a kind of cloth swing*?

   Ⓐ hammer   Ⓒ hammock   Ⓔ none
   Ⓑ ham   Ⓓ hamper

2. Which word comes from the Latin <u>locus</u>, meaning *place*?

   Ⓐ local   Ⓒ lock   Ⓔ none
   Ⓑ locate   Ⓓ look

3. Which word comes from the Old English <u>sceo</u>, meaning *cloud*?

   Ⓐ school   Ⓒ scene   Ⓔ none
   Ⓑ sky   Ⓓ skew

4. Which word comes from the Latin <u>addenda</u>, meaning *things put on*?

   Ⓐ addition Ⓒ addict Ⓔ none
   Ⓑ adder   Ⓓ addle

5. Which word comes from <u>Gaea</u>, the Greek goddess of the earth?

   Ⓐ general   Ⓒ geography Ⓔ none
   Ⓑ games   Ⓓ gaze

6. Which word comes from the name <u>John Duns Scotus</u>, whose writings were made fun of in the 16th century?

   Ⓐ dunk   Ⓒ dune   Ⓔ none
   Ⓑ dunce   Ⓓ dupe

7. Which word comes from <u>Hypnos</u>, the Greek god of sleep?

   Ⓐ hype   Ⓒ hymn   Ⓔ none
   Ⓑ hydrant Ⓓ hyena

8. Which word comes from the French <u>domestique</u>, meaning *household or family*?

   Ⓐ domino   Ⓒ dominate Ⓔ none
   Ⓑ domestic Ⓓ dome

Your time:_____

Number right:_____

Unit Two: Vocabulary

Name _____   Date _____

Lesson 3: Thinking about word relationships
Part one

DIRECTIONS ▶ Darken the circle for the word that means <u>the same</u> or <u>almost the same</u> as the underlined word in each sentence. Darken *E none* if the correct answer is <u>not given</u>.

STRATEGY TIPS

1. Read each sentence carefully.
2. Remember that you are looking for words that have similar meanings to the underlined words.

Sample:
We were <u>apprehensive</u> about going into the empty house.

- Ⓐ happy
- Ⓑ fearful
- Ⓒ hostile
- Ⓓ annoyed
- Ⓔ none

ANSWER

The correct answer is *B fearful*. Someone who is *apprehensive* about doing something is anxious or worried about it. All four choices fit in the sentence, but only *fearful* means almost the same as *apprehensive*.

NOW TRY THESE

1. We all thought that Sandy was a <u>charming</u> story-teller.
   - Ⓐ delightful
   - Ⓑ silly
   - Ⓒ funny
   - Ⓓ serious
   - Ⓔ none

2. The tornado <u>destroyed</u> many homes.
   - Ⓐ finished
   - Ⓑ flooded
   - Ⓒ demolished
   - Ⓓ demonstrated
   - Ⓔ none

3. Matti's teacher <u>encouraged</u> her to enter the contest.
   - Ⓐ urged
   - Ⓑ engaged
   - Ⓒ saved
   - Ⓓ employed
   - Ⓔ none

4. Please give me your <u>candid</u> opinion about my book.
   - Ⓐ divine
   - Ⓑ honest
   - Ⓒ loud
   - Ⓓ only
   - Ⓔ none

5. Kim's drawings are always filled with <u>fanciful</u> designs.
   - Ⓐ famous
   - Ⓑ fair
   - Ⓒ imaginative
   - Ⓓ imperative
   - Ⓔ none

6. Celebrities are often considered good <u>models</u> for young people.
   - Ⓐ drivers
   - Ⓑ actors
   - Ⓒ clerks
   - Ⓓ examples
   - Ⓔ none

GO ON TO NEXT PAGE

Name_____ Date_____

Part two

DIRECTIONS ▶ Darken the circle for the word that is the opposite of the underlined word. Darken *E none* if the correct answer is not given.

Sample:
Sammy likes to collect <u>rare</u> stamps.

- Ⓐ beautiful
- Ⓑ foreign
- Ⓒ ordinary
- Ⓓ historic
- Ⓔ none

ANSWER

The correct answer is *C ordinary*. All of the choices would fit the sentence, but only *ordinary* has the opposite meaning of *rare*.

NOW TRY THESE

7. We watched the acrobat with <u>amazement</u>.
   - Ⓐ awe
   - Ⓑ surprise
   - Ⓒ admiration
   - Ⓓ indifference
   - Ⓔ none

8. Our school librarian is a really <u>amiable</u> person.
   - Ⓐ kind
   - Ⓑ charming
   - Ⓒ churlish
   - Ⓓ gentle
   - Ⓔ none

9. The officer's clothes looked <u>neat</u> and clean.
   - Ⓐ slovenly
   - Ⓑ prim
   - Ⓒ dapper
   - Ⓓ tidy
   - Ⓔ none

10. We enjoyed visiting the <u>rustic</u> homes of the early settlers.
    - Ⓐ rural
    - Ⓑ awkward
    - Ⓒ coarse
    - Ⓓ elegant
    - Ⓔ none

11. The tickets for that show were less than the <u>usual</u> price.
    - Ⓐ everyday
    - Ⓑ regular
    - Ⓒ general
    - Ⓓ familiar
    - Ⓔ none

12. Vinnie is <u>determined</u> to learn the computer this year.
    - Ⓐ resolved
    - Ⓑ deciding
    - Ⓒ hesitant
    - Ⓓ sure
    - Ⓔ none

13. She is the most <u>talkative</u> person I know.
    - Ⓐ chatty
    - Ⓑ remote
    - Ⓒ friendly
    - Ⓓ loud
    - Ⓔ none

STOP

Your time:_____

Number right:_____

Name_____ Date_____

Lesson 4: Homographs—words with more than one meaning

DIRECTIONS ▸ Darken the circle for the word that fits both meanings.

1. Homographs are words that are spelled alike but have different meanings and, sometimes, different pronunciations.
2. Read the underlined definitions carefully.
3. Choose the one word that will fit both meanings.

Sample:

a section of an army
a mathematical operation

Ⓐ addition   Ⓒ division
Ⓑ algebra   Ⓓ troop

ANSWER

The correct answer is *C division*. *Division* is the only word that fits both definitions.

1. to look curiously or closely
   a person of the same rank; an equal

   Ⓐ stare   Ⓒ gaze
   Ⓑ friend Ⓓ peer

2. the sound a dog makes
   the covering on a tree

   Ⓐ yelp   Ⓒ leaves
   Ⓑ bark   Ⓓ whimper

3. to argue against or be opposed to
   something that can be seen or felt

   Ⓐ toy   Ⓒ speak
   Ⓑ vote   Ⓓ object

4. a kind of blue-gray stone
   a list of candidates for office

   Ⓐ slate   Ⓒ panel
   Ⓑ rock   Ⓓ choice

5. an injury or hurt
   past tense of *wind*

   Ⓐ scar   Ⓒ cut
   Ⓑ wend   Ⓓ wound

6. a group of workers
   a pole or stick used for support

   Ⓐ team   Ⓒ staff
   Ⓑ post   Ⓓ club

Your time:_____

Number right:_____

Name_____   Date _____

Lesson 5: Using context clues

DIRECTIONS ▸ Darken the circle for the word that best fits each sentence in the paragraphs.

STRATEGY TIPS

1. Use the context, all the words in the sentences, to help you decide which word makes sense in each sentence.
2. Remember that all the choices will fit the sentence, but only one word will make the most sense.

Sample:

When we send __(S1)__ back and forth, we are communicating. We are sharing __(S2)__ and ideas.

S1 Ⓐ packages   Ⓑ games   Ⓒ people   Ⓓ messages
S2 Ⓐ information Ⓑ food   Ⓒ paper   Ⓓ songs

ANSWER

The correct answer for S1 is *D messages*. The correct answer for S2 is *A information*. When we communicate we send *messages*, not *packages*, *people*, or *games*. The messages contain *information*.

NOW TRY THESE

Most large cities have beautiful __(1)__ for their citizens. People like to enjoy them in good __(2)__.

1. Ⓐ museums   Ⓑ statues   Ⓒ parks   Ⓓ buildings
2. Ⓐ times   Ⓑ weather   Ⓒ ways   Ⓓ storms

Hurricanes can cause a great deal of __(3)__. They can affect water supply and electricity. Without electricity there is no __(4)__, and food can quickly spoil.

3. Ⓐ heat   Ⓑ damage   Ⓒ storms   Ⓓ parties
4. Ⓐ fuel   Ⓑ phone   Ⓒ refrigeration Ⓓ wind

Maple syrup is made from the sap of maple trees. The syrup is collected when the daytime __(5)__ goes above freezing and __(6)__ below freezing in the nighttime.

5. Ⓐ sun   Ⓑ rain   Ⓒ temperature   Ⓓ storm
6. Ⓐ drops   Ⓑ waits   Ⓒ calls   Ⓓ lasts

GO ON TO NEXT PAGE

Name_____ Date _____

Unit II, lesson 5, page 2

Coaches were used for transportation by royal families. The coaches were usually decorated with __(7)__ to show the family's wealth to other people. However, because there were no springs, coach rides were not very __(8)__.

7. Ⓐ names   Ⓑ valuables   Ⓒ vines   Ⓓ palaces
8. Ⓐ long   Ⓑ happy   Ⓒ comfortable Ⓓ dangerous

Some of our past __(9)__ are honored in a special way in Washington, D.C. George Washington, Thomas Jefferson, and Abraham Lincoln each have a __(10)__ in their honor.

9. Ⓐ presidents Ⓑ princes   Ⓒ mayors   Ⓓ citizens
10. Ⓐ magazine   Ⓑ mansion   Ⓒ monument Ⓓ mausoleum

Nonfiction is a form of literature that includes many types of writing. Some of these types are essays, __(11)__ , and articles. The basic difference between fiction and nonfiction is that nonfiction is concerned with __(12)__ facts, ideas, and events.

11. Ⓐ songs   Ⓑ poems   Ⓒ riddles   Ⓓ biographies
12. Ⓐ imaginary Ⓑ true   Ⓒ ridiculous Ⓓ vague

STOP

Your time: _____

Number right: _____

On this lesson I did _____ because _____

_____.

I think it would help me to _____

_____

_____.

PRACTICE TEST 2

Part 1

Directions: For questions 1-4, darken the circle on the answer sheet for the letter of the word that completes the analogy. Darken the circle for *E none* if the correct answer is not given.

Sample: white : snow = gray : _____

A river D summer
B sun E none
C fog

Answer: The correct answer is *C fog*. We usually think of *fog* as being gray.

1. sculpture : stone = watercolor : _____
   A paper D plaster
   B wood E none
   C metal

2. swarm : bee = flock : _____
   A ants D cattle
   B sheep E none
   C gaggle

3. clue : through = though : _____
   A few D flow
   B new E none
   C bough

4. precise : careless = riddle : _____
   A answer D problem
   B puzzle E none
   C mystery

Part 2

Directions: For questions 5-8, darken the circle on the answer sheet for the letter of the word that comes from another language. Darken the circle for *E none* if the correct answer is not given.

Sample: Which word comes from the Italian <u>ballotta</u>, a small ball used to register to vote?

A ball D ballast
B balloon E none
C ballot

Answer: The correct answer is *C ballot*. A *ballot* is used to register a vote.

Name_____ Date _____

Test Two: Vocabulary

Practice test 2, part 2, page 2

5. Which word comes from the Dutch <u>koekje</u>, a little cake?
   A corn   D cookie
   B candy   E none
   C condiment

6. Which word comes from the Japanese <u>hancho</u>, a squad leader?
   A handle   D handsome
   B honcho   E none
   C hangman

7. Which word comes from the Arabic <u>sifr</u>, meaning *empty*?
   A zero   D zombie
   B zing   E none
   C zap

8. Which word comes from the Latin <u>custos</u>, meaning *guardian or watchman*?
   A customary D costume
   B custodian E none
   C customer

Part 3

Directions: For questions 9-12, darken the circle on the answer sheet for the letter of the word that means the <u>same</u> or <u>almost the same</u> as the underlined word in each sentence. Darken *E none* if the answer is <u>not given</u>.

Sample: We had to <u>shorten</u> our vacation time because of the hurricane.
   A delay   D detail
   B decrease   E none
   C defer

Answer: The correct answer is *B decrease*. To *decrease* is to make less.

9. Everyone was asked to <u>contribute</u> toys for the holiday party.
   A buy   D deliver
   B collect   E none
   C donate

10. Referees should try to be <u>impartial</u>.
    A timely   D appropriate
    B kind   E none
    C right

© Steck-Vaughn Company

25

Test Taking 6, SV 6774-3

Practice test 2, part 3, page 2

11. Some children are very <u>inquisitive</u>—they want to know how everything works.

   A bothersome D happy
   B curious   E none
   C silly

12. The tailor <u>altered</u> the sleeves on Suni's jacket.

   A started   D cut
   B designed E none
   C changed

Part 4

Directions: For questions 13-16, darken the circle on the answer sheet for the letter of the word that means the <u>opposite</u> of the underlined word in each sentence. Darken *E none* if the correct word is <u>not given</u>.

Sample: I <u>doubt</u> that the plane will arrive on time.

   A think   D hope
   B see   E none
   C believe

Answer: The correct answer is *C believe*. To doubt is to question; *believe* is the opposite of *doubt*.

13. The farmer raised an <u>abundant</u> crop of vegetables.

   A scarce   D bumper
   B beautiful E none
   C varied

14. Isabel has a very <u>pleasant</u> personality.

   A agreeable D sunny
   B enormous   E none
   C obnoxious

15. Leonard is a <u>capable</u> musician.

   A careful D charming
   B awkward E none
   C serious

16. The party turned out to be an enormous <u>fiasco</u>.

   A success   D complication
   B problem   E none
   C disaster

Part 5

Directions: For questions 17-18, darken the circle on the answer sheet for the letter of the word that fits both meanings.

Sample: a color
             inexperienced or new

   A green   C black
   B blue   D white

Answer: The correct answer is *A green*.

GO ON TO NEXT PAGE

Name_____ Date _____

Practice test 2, part 5, page 2

17. <u>a frame of metal bars</u>
    <u>to rub into small particles</u>
    - **A** fireplace
    - **B** saw
    - **C** grate
    - **D** window

18. <u>a pit from which minerals are taken</u>
    <u>belonging to me</u>
    - **A** dig
    - **B** mine
    - **C** coal
    - **D** I

Part 6

Directions: For questions 19-22, darken the circle on the answer sheet for the letter of the word that best completes the sentences in the paragraphs below.

Sample: Norway is a long, narrow country. It is __(S1)__ next to Sweden. Norway has many __(S2)__ which rise steeply from the western shore.

S1   A labeled   B located   C contained   D extended
S2   A rivers   B lakes   C cities   D mountains

Answer: The correct answer for S1 is *B located*. The correct answer for S2 is *D mountains*.

Whenever you see a map in your textbook, look at the __(19)__ first. This will tell you what is being shown on the map. Then look at the __(20)__, or key. This will tell you the size, distance, or number of what is being shown.

19. **A** colors   **B** title   **C** direction   **D** lines
20. **A** diagram   **B** equator   **C** direction   **D** legend

Information texts convey knowledge about a topic. Standardized test questions are used to determine how well readers __(21)__ the material. Often there are questions about the __(22)__ found in charts, graphs, or maps.

21. **A** like   **B** understand   **C** fail   **D** draw
22. **A** pictures   **B** designs   **C** skills **D** information

STOP

Suggested Time Limit: 25 minutes   Your time: _____
Check your work if you have time. Wait for instructions from your teacher.

Name _____ Date _____

UNIT III: GRAMMAR PRACTICE

Lesson 1: Identifying nouns, verbs, and pronouns

DIRECTIONS ▶ Darken the circle for the word that is a noun, verb, or pronoun. Darken *E none* if the correct answer is *not given*.

STRATEGY TIPS
1. Remember that nouns usually name the subject of a sentence. Nouns can be common, proper, or plural.
2. Pronouns are used in place of nouns.
3. Verbs show action or being

Sample:
Which word is a verb?
Will you please close the door?
   Ⓐ   Ⓑ   Ⓒ   Ⓓ   Ⓔ none

ANSWER
The correct answer is *D close*. A verb tells what a subject does. *Close* tells the subject what to do.

NOW TRY THESE

1. Which word is a pronoun?
   The children waved their flags when the parade went by.
        Ⓐ   Ⓑ   Ⓒ   Ⓓ   Ⓔ none

2. Which word is a verb?
   We are thinking about going to the movies tonight.
           Ⓐ   Ⓑ   Ⓒ   Ⓓ   Ⓔ none

3. Which word is a plural noun?
   All the children in our class passed the test.
    Ⓐ   Ⓑ   Ⓒ   Ⓓ   Ⓔ none

4. Which word is a proper noun?
   The scout troop went camping in Canada last summer.
          Ⓐ   Ⓑ   Ⓒ   Ⓓ   Ⓔ none

5. Which word is a plural noun?
   Students should use a dictionary to check spelling errors.
    Ⓐ   Ⓑ   Ⓒ   Ⓓ   Ⓔ none

Your time: _____
Number right: _____

Unit Three: Grammar Practice

Name_____ Date_____

Lesson 2: Identifying adjectives and adverbs

 Darken the circle for the word that is an adverb or an adjective. Darken *E none* if the correct answer is not given.

STRATEGY TIPS
1. Adjectives change, limit, or describe persons, places, or things.
2. Adverbs describe verbs. They tell how, when, and where something is being done.

Sample:
Which word is an adjective?
That sofa looks very comfortable
    Ⓐ   Ⓑ   Ⓒ   Ⓓ   Ⓔ none

ANSWER
The correct answer is
D *comfortable*. *Comfortable*
describes the sofa.

 **NOW TRY THESE**

1. Which word is an adjective?
   The crayon left a blue stain on my blouse.
      Ⓐ   Ⓑ Ⓒ   Ⓓ   Ⓔ none

2. Which word is an adverb?
   Melinda returned her library books yesterday.
      Ⓐ   Ⓑ   Ⓒ Ⓓ   Ⓔ none

3. Which word is an adverb?
   The runaway horse really frightened us.
       Ⓐ   Ⓑ   Ⓒ   Ⓓ   Ⓔ none

4. Which word is an adjective?
   Maine's rocky coast attracts many visitors.
      Ⓐ   Ⓑ   Ⓒ   Ⓓ   Ⓔ none

5. Which word is an adverb?
   Our classroom is decorated very nicely with bright colors.
      Ⓐ   Ⓑ   Ⓒ   Ⓓ   Ⓔ none

6. Which word is an adjective?
   You need to use measuring cups to get good baking results.
      Ⓐ   Ⓑ   Ⓒ Ⓓ Ⓔ none

Your time:_____
Number right:_____

© Steck-Vaughn Company
Test Taking 6, SV 6774-3

Name_____ Date _____

Lesson 3: Identifying conjunctions and prepositions

DIRECTIONS ▶ Darken the circle for the word that is a preposition or a conjunction. Darken *E none* if the correct answer is not given.

STRATEGY TIPS

1. When you look at a sentence, think about how the words are connected or joined.
2. A conjunction is a word that joins words, phrases, or clauses.
3. Prepositions connect nouns and pronouns to other words in a sentence.

Sample:
Which word is a conjunction?
Aunt Sylvia <u>sent</u> my sister <u>and</u> me <u>beautiful</u> gifts <u>for</u> Christmas.
          (A)   (B)   (C)   (D)   (E) none

ANSWER | The correct answer is *B and*. *And* joins the two subjects, "my sister" and "me."

NOW TRY THESE

1. Which word is a conjunction?
   Would you <u>prefer</u> to <u>see</u> a movie <u>or</u> watch television?
     (A)   (B)   (C)   (D)   (E) none

2. Which word is a preposition?
   We <u>found</u> the <u>campsite</u> <u>without</u> any <u>trouble</u>.
     (A)   (B)   (C)   (D)   (E) none

3. Which word is a preposition?
   People <u>travel</u> <u>beneath</u> the <u>streets</u> when <u>they</u> <u>use</u> the subway.
     (A)   (B)   (C)(D)   (E) none

4. Which word is a preposition?
   The traffic jam <u>caused</u> us to <u>miss</u> the <u>beginning</u> <u>of</u> the concert.
     (A)   (B)   (C)   (D)   (E) none

5. Which word is a conjunction?
   Angie <u>wanted</u> to buy <u>computer</u> software, <u>so</u> she <u>saved</u> her allowance.
     (A)   (B)   (C)   (D)   (E) none

6. Which word is a conjunction?
   Brian <u>always</u> does <u>his</u> work <u>quickly</u> <u>but</u> carefully.
     (A)   (B)   (C) (D)   (E) none

STOP

Your time:_____
Number right:_____

Name_____ Date _____

Lesson 4: Identifying simple, compound, and complex sentences

DIRECTIONS Read each sentence. Decide whether it is simple, compound, complex, or a sentence fragment. Write the letter that answers the question.

STRATEGY TIPS
1. Think about the grammatical structure of sentences.
2. A simple sentence is made up of one independent clause.
3. A compound sentence is made up of two or more independent clauses which can be joined by a coordinating conjunction or a semicolon.
4. A complex sentence is made by joining an independent clause to a dependent clause.
5. Sentence fragments are incomplete sentences.

Sample:
____ Choose the correct label for the following sentence.
I hung my coat in the closet, and I went to my room.

ⓐ compound   ⓑ complex   ⓒ simple   ⓓ sentence fragment

ANSWER
The correct answer is *A compound*. The two clauses are joined by the conjunction *and*.

NOW TRY THESE

Use the choices below to label the following sentences.

ⓐ compound   ⓑ complex   ⓒ simple   ⓓ sentence fragment

_____ 1. Sandy ran to the playground; he didn't want to miss the game.
_____ 2. The kids ran and jumped through the waves.
_____ 3. When my dog gets to know you, he stops barking.
_____ 4. After I got home.
_____ 5. The girl who sits in front of me.
_____ 6. We have to go to the supermarket because we are out of food.
_____ 7. Ray tried out for the team, but he didn't make it.
_____ 8. Keith always rooted for the Orioles until they left the league.
_____ 9. After the movie, we went out to eat.
_____ 10. Are Buddy and Fritz best friends?

Your time:_____
Number right:_____

Name_____ Date_____

PRACTICE TEST 3

Part 1

Directions: For questions 1-4, darken the circle on the answer sheet for the letter of the word that is a noun, a verb, or a pronoun. Darken *E none* if the correct answer is <u>not given</u>.

Sample: Which word is a pronoun?
Christine and Maria invited us to a holiday party.
     A   B   C   D   E none

Answer: The correct answer is *C us.*

1. Which of the following words is a verb?
Maria is the tallest girl in the class.
    A B   C   D   E none

2. Which of the following words is a noun?
Each of the women baked a pie for the class picnic.
  A   B   C   D   E none

3. Which of the following words is a pronoun?
The children washed their hands before lunch.
    A   B   C D   E none

4. Which of the following words is a noun?
Next year we will start to learn Spanish.
   A   B   C   D   E none

Part 2

Directions: For questions 5-8, darken the circle on the answer sheet for the letter of the word that is an adjective or an adverb. Darken *E none* if the correct answer is <u>not given</u>.

Sample: Which word is an adjective?
Valerie bought a new sweater at the mall.
        A   B   C   D E none

Answer: The correct answer is *B new.*

Name _____ Date _____

Practice test 3, part 2, page 2

5. Which word is an adverb?
   <u>Morgan</u> will <u>visit</u> us <u>later</u> this <u>afternoon</u>.
      A   B   C   D   E none

6. Which word is an adverb?
   I <u>sit</u> in this <u>seat</u>; <u>Sally</u> sits <u>there</u>.
      A   B   C   D   E none

7. Which word is an adjective?
   The <u>lucky</u> woman <u>won</u> the <u>lottery</u> last <u>week</u>.
      A   B   C   D   E none

8. Which word is an adverb?
   <u>Countries</u> near the <u>equator</u> have <u>extremely</u> <u>hot</u> weather.
      A   B   C   D   E none

Part 3

Directions: For questions 9-12, darken the letter on the answer sheet of the word that is a conjunction or a preposition. Darken *E none* if the correct answer is <u>not</u> given.

Sample: Which word is a conjunction?
We <u>wanted</u> to go <u>for</u> a ride, <u>but</u> we <u>had</u> a flat tire.
    A   B   C   D   E none

Answer: The correct answer is *C but*.

9. Which word is a preposition?
   Nina <u>keeps</u> <u>all</u> her <u>stuffed</u> animals <u>on</u> a shelf.
      A B   C   D   E none

10. Which word is a preposition?
    They <u>had</u> to put a <u>cover</u> <u>over</u> the field <u>when</u> it <u>started</u> to rain.
        A   B   C   D E none

Name _____ Date _____

Test Three: Grammar Practice

Practice test 3, part 3, page 2

11. Which word is a conjunction?
    You <u>can</u> use <u>e-mail</u> <u>or</u> the post office to <u>send</u> a letter.
       A   B   C   D   E none

12. Which word is a conjunction?
    It was getting <u>very</u> cold, <u>so</u> we went <u>back</u> for our <u>sweaters</u>.
                  A   B   C   D   E none

Part 4

Directions: For questions 13-20, darken the circle on the answer sheet for the word that tells whether a sentence is simple, compound, complex, or a sentence fragment.

Sample: Choose the correct label for the sentence.
Our teacher showed Donnie and me how to solve the problem.

    A compound   **B** simple   **C** complex   **D** fragment

Answer: The correct answer is *B simple*.

Use the choices below to label each sentence.

A compound   **B** simple   **C** complex   **D** fragment

13. Sara Jean is only eleven, yet she can read her sister's high school books.

14. The new computer, which they just bought, has a lot of good software.

15. Anybody who plays tennis.

16. Juan is very unhappy because his best friend is moving.

17. We need to buy more supplies or we won't be able to finish the project.

18. My favorite program.

19. Who was the last one to use the scissors?

20. Frank, who lives near me, is a good chess player.

Suggested Time Limit: 24 minutes   Your time: _____
Check your work if you have time. Wait for instructions from your teacher.

Name_____ Date_____

UNIT IV: LANGUAGE USAGE

Lesson 1: Identifying correct spelling
Part one

DIRECTIONS ▶ Darken the circle for the correctly spelled word.

STRATEGY TIPS

1. Study the choices carefully.
2. Decide which choices are wrong, then pick the word that looks right to you.

Sample:
I _____ want to read that book.

    Ⓐ definitely   Ⓒ definitly
    Ⓑ definately   Ⓓ defanitely

ANSWER
The correct spelling is A *definitely*. The other words may sound like *definitely*, but they are wrong.

NOW TRY THESE

1. We couldn't _____ the magic tricks that Phillip showed us.
   Ⓐ bilieve   Ⓒ believe
   Ⓑ beleive   Ⓓ bilieve

2. Pepe is planning to swim _____ laps tomorrow.
   Ⓐ fourty   Ⓒ forety
   Ⓑ forty   Ⓓ fortey

3. The stars were _____ brightly in the sky.
   Ⓐ shineing   Ⓒ shinning
   Ⓑ shining   Ⓓ shinneing

4. Bella ordered a tuna fish _____ for lunch.
   Ⓐ sanwich   Ⓒ sanawich
   Ⓑ sandwhich   Ⓓ sandwich

Part two

DIRECTIONS ▶ Darken the circle for the word that is misspelled.

Sample: Ⓐ comeing   Ⓑ course   Ⓒ coming   Ⓓ chose

Answer: The correct answer is *A comeing*. The other words are all spelled correctly.

NOW TRY THESE

5. Ⓐ busy   Ⓑ busted   Ⓒ buseniss   Ⓓ bustle
6. Ⓐ label   Ⓑ laboratory   Ⓒ labyrinth   Ⓓ laboriius
7. Ⓐ principel   Ⓑ principal   Ⓒ principle   Ⓓ principality
8. Ⓐ sinister   Ⓑ sincerity   Ⓒ sinserely   Ⓓ singular

Your time:_____ Number right:_____

Unit Four: Language Usage

Name_____ Date_____

Lesson 2: Identifying correct capitalization and punctuation

Part one

DIRECTIONS ▸ Darken the circle for the part of the sentence that should be capitalized. Darken *E none* if no capital letter is neccessary.

STRATEGY TIPS

Use capitals: 1. in the first word of a sentence.
2. in the first word of a quotation.
3. in proper nouns (people's names, holidays, place names).
4. in key words of titles and in names of languages.

Sample: Last July   we visited   the Grand canyon   in Arizona.
Ⓐ   Ⓑ   Ⓒ   Ⓓ   Ⓔ none

Answer: The correct answer is *C the Grand canyon.* All parts of a place name should start with a capital.

NOW TRY THESE

1. The post office   is on   stewart Avenue   in Middletown.
Ⓐ   Ⓑ   Ⓒ   Ⓓ   Ⓔ none

2. We're planning to   eat Mexican   food when we   meet Jim tonight.
Ⓐ   Ⓑ   Ⓒ   Ⓓ   Ⓔ none

3. On Election day   we vote   for the people   who make our laws.
Ⓐ   Ⓑ   Ⓒ   Ⓓ   Ⓔ none

Part two

DIRECTIONS ▸ Darken the circle for the punctuation mark that makes the sentence correct. Darken *E none* if no punctuation is necessary.

Sample: She asked, "Why did you do that"
Ⓐ !   Ⓑ :   Ⓒ ?   Ⓓ ;   Ⓔ none

Answer: The correct answer is *C ?.* This mark must be used at the end of a question.

NOW TRY THESE

4. *The Ugly Duckling,* by Hans Christian Anderson, is my favorite fairy tale.
Ⓐ ?   Ⓑ "   Ⓒ ,   Ⓓ ;   Ⓔ none

5. It is ten below zero outside!
Ⓐ .   Ⓑ ;   Ⓒ '   Ⓓ "   Ⓔ none

STOP

Your time:_____   Number right:_____

Unit Four: Language Usage

Name_____   Date_____

Lesson 3: Proofreading compositions

DIRECTIONS ▶ Read all the sentences in the composition, then darken the circle for the correct answer to each question.

STRATEGY TIPS

Pretend that you are an editor. Think about all the rules you know for punctuation, capitalization, spelling, word usage, and sentence structure. Answer the questions using those rules.

Sample: George Washington had more than one career. He was a surveyor, a
　　　　　　　　　　　　　　　　(1)　　　　　　　　　　　　　　　　　(2)
soldier, and a statesman and a president. First he was a surveyor.
　　　　　　　　　　　　　　　　　　　　　　　(3)
During the Revolutionary War, he was a general.
　　(4)

Which is the best way to write sentence 2?

Ⓐ He was a surveyor and a soldier and a statesman and was a president.
Ⓑ He was a surveyor, a soldier, a statesman, and a president.
Ⓒ He was a surveyor; a soldier and a statesman, and a president.
Ⓓ As it is written.

Answer: The correct answer is *B*. Use commas between more than two items in a series.

NOW TRY THESE

　　Our survival depends on our atmosphere without the atmosphere our earth would
　　　　　　　　　　　　　　(1)
be a dry barren desert. We wouldn't be able to survive without an atmosphere.
　　　　　　　　　　　　　　　　　　(2)
We need the atmospheres's oxygen to breathe. And the water cycle too.
　　　(3)　　　　　　　　　　　　　　　　　　　　　(4)
　　Food growth also depends upon our atmosphere. Plants which receive water
　　　(5)　　　　　　　　　　　　　　　　　　　　　　　(6)
carbon dioxide, and sunlight could not survive without the atmosphere. Without the
atmosphere, the animals that provide us with food could not exist.
　　　　　　　　　　　　　　(7)

1. Which is the topic sentence in the second paragraph?
　　Ⓐ 7　　　　Ⓑ 5　　　　Ⓒ 4　　　　Ⓓ 6

2. Which sentence has a spelling error?
　　Ⓐ 2　　　　Ⓑ 4　　　　Ⓒ 3　　　　Ⓓ none

3. Which sentence has a punctuation error?
　　Ⓐ 6　　　　Ⓑ 7　　　　Ⓒ 5　　　　Ⓓ none

GO ON TO NEXT PAGE ▶

Name_____   Date_____

Unit IV, lesson 3, page 2

4. Which sentence is a run-on sentence?
   - Ⓐ 1
   - Ⓑ 3
   - Ⓒ 5
   - Ⓓ none

5. Which is a sentence fragment?
   - Ⓐ 7
   - Ⓑ 4
   - Ⓒ 2
   - Ⓓ none

6. Which is the best way to write sentence 5?
   - Ⓐ Food growth, also depends upon our atmosphere.
   - Ⓑ Food growth also, depends upon our atmosphere.
   - Ⓒ Food growth also depends upon, our atmosphere.
   - Ⓓ As it is written.

Our <u>lives are influence by</u> the atmosphere in many ways. First, the condition of the
       (8)
<u>atmosphere called climate</u> determines what clothes we wear. If the climate is very
        (9)
<u>warm, a person</u> would wear light-weight clothing. Secondly, <u>the style of homes are</u>
     (10)   (11)
influenced by climate. The <u>choices of building material are determined</u> by the climate.
                                              (12)
Thirdly, <u>climate even influenced</u> the sports we play and where we play them. Even our
              (13)
<u>mood of transportation</u> is influenced by climate.
       (14)

7. In sentence 8, <u>lives are influence by</u> is best written
   - Ⓐ lives is influence by
   - Ⓑ lives are influenced by
   - Ⓒ live are influence by
   - Ⓓ as it is written

8. Which sentence has an incorrectly used word?
   - Ⓐ 14
   - Ⓑ 12
   - Ⓒ 11
   - Ⓓ none

9. In sentence 9, <u>atmosphere called climate</u> is best written
   - Ⓐ atmosphere, called climate
   - Ⓑ atmosphere called, climate
   - Ⓒ atmosphere, called climate,
   - Ⓓ as it is written

10. In sentence 11, <u>the style of homes are</u> is best written
    - Ⓐ the styles of homes is
    - Ⓑ the style of homes is
    - Ⓒ the styles of houses is
    - Ⓓ as it is written

Your time:_____
Number right:_____

Unit Four: Language Usage

Name_____ Date_____

Lesson 4: Identifying complete subjects and predicates

DIRECTIONS ▶ Darken the circle for the choice that shows the complete subject or the complete predicate of the sentence.

STRATEGY TIPS

1. The complete subject is the subject and all the words that tell about it in a sentence.
2. The complete predicate is the verb and any words about it.

Sample: Evan and Kerry went to a pool party.

S1 Which is the complete subject?
- Ⓐ Maria
- Ⓑ Evan
- Ⓒ Evan and Kerry
- Ⓓ Kerry

S2 Which is the complete predicate?
- Ⓐ pool party
- Ⓑ went to a pool party
- Ⓒ Maria's house
- Ⓓ went to

ANSWER

S1 The correct answer is *C Evan and Kerry*. The sentence is about Evan and Kerry.

S2 The correct answer is *B went to a pool party*. This tells what the subjects did.

NOW TRY THESE

1. What is the complete subject of this sentence?
   All of the children wore red ribbons on their jackets.
   - Ⓐ children wore
   - Ⓑ All of the children
   - Ⓒ red ribbons
   - Ⓓ their jackets

2. What is the complete predicate of this sentence?
   My new sneakers are black and white.
   - Ⓐ are black and white
   - Ⓑ new sneakers
   - Ⓒ My new
   - Ⓓ sneakers are black and white

3. What is the complete predicate of this sentence?
   The truck driver drove down the new highway.
   - Ⓐ The truck driver
   - Ⓑ driver drove
   - Ⓒ drove down the new highway
   - Ⓓ new highway

4. What is the complete subject of this sentence?
   All my friends are going on the class trip next week.
   - Ⓐ the class trip
   - Ⓑ All my friends
   - Ⓒ friends are going
   - Ⓓ trip next week

5. What is the complete subject of this sentence?
   The storm destroyed all the vegetables in our garden.
   - Ⓐ vegetables in our garden
   - Ⓑ storm destroyed
   - Ⓒ all the vegetables
   - Ⓓ The storm

Your time:_____ Number right:_____

Name_____ Date_____

Lesson 5: Practicing with pronouns
Part one

DIRECTIONS ▶ Darken the circle for the pronoun that completes the sentence. Darken the circle for *E none* if the correct choice is <u>not given</u>.

STRATEGY TIPS
1. A pronoun is a word that is used in place of a noun.
2. An antecedent is the noun to which the pronoun refers.
3. Pronouns may be subjects, objects, or possessives.

Sample: Kirstie and ____ went shopping after school.

Ⓐ me Ⓓ her
Ⓑ us Ⓔ none
Ⓒ I

ANSWER
The correct answer is *C I. Kirstie and I* are the subjects of this sentence, so a subject form pronoun must be used.

NOW TRY THESE

1. You and ____ are the best dancers in our class.
   Ⓐ them Ⓓ us
   Ⓑ their Ⓔ none
   Ⓒ they

2. Which jacket is ____?
   Ⓐ your Ⓓ its
   Ⓑ hers Ⓔ none
   Ⓒ you're

3. Lucy and ____ are best friends.
   Ⓐ she Ⓓ him
   Ⓑ her Ⓔ none
   Ⓒ them

4. Tobie's father is taking ____ on a camping trip.
   Ⓐ we Ⓓ he
   Ⓑ they Ⓔ none
   Ⓒ him

5. If it weren't for ____, we would never have found the keys.
   Ⓐ she Ⓓ they
   Ⓑ he Ⓔ none
   Ⓒ my

6. The soccer team held a car wash to raise money for ____ new uniforms.
   Ⓐ they're Ⓓ them
   Ⓑ their Ⓔ none
   Ⓒ there

7. Jerry and ____ almost missed the school bus this morning.
   Ⓐ her Ⓓ us
   Ⓑ him Ⓔ none
   Ⓒ I

8. My grandmother baked cookies for Eddie and ____.
   Ⓐ we Ⓓ they
   Ⓑ she Ⓔ none
   Ⓒ he

GO ON TO NEXT PAGE

Unit Four: Language Usage

Name _____ Date _____

Part two

DIRECTIONS ▶ Darken the circle for the pronoun that can replace the underlined word or words in the sentence. Darken *E none* if the correct choice is not given.

NOW TRY THESE

9. I showed <u>Sylvie</u> my new winter boots.
    - Ⓐ she
    - Ⓑ her
    - Ⓒ we
    - Ⓓ his
    - Ⓔ none

10. George told <u>Phil</u> that he could ride to school with them.
    - Ⓐ them
    - Ⓑ him
    - Ⓒ she
    - Ⓓ he
    - Ⓔ none

11. <u>Lana and Hope</u> are planning to start a camera club.
    - Ⓐ We
    - Ⓑ They
    - Ⓒ Us
    - Ⓓ Them
    - Ⓔ none

12. Always wait until the cake cools before you put icing on <u>the cake</u>.
    - Ⓐ its
    - Ⓑ our
    - Ⓒ it
    - Ⓓ me
    - Ⓔ none

13. We are all going with Chet to visit <u>Chet's</u> grandparents' farm.
    - Ⓐ their
    - Ⓑ his
    - Ⓒ our
    - Ⓓ them
    - Ⓔ none

14. <u>My brothers and my mother</u> go to an exercise class every morning.
    - Ⓐ Us
    - Ⓑ They
    - Ⓒ Our
    - Ⓓ Their
    - Ⓔ none

15. Jimmy's father wants <u>Jimmy</u> to mow the lawn tomorrow morning.
    - Ⓐ he
    - Ⓑ him
    - Ⓒ his
    - Ⓓ me
    - Ⓔ none

16. It was <u>Louise</u> who won the spelling bee.
    - Ⓐ you
    - Ⓑ your
    - Ⓒ she
    - Ⓓ her
    - Ⓔ none

STOP

Your time: _____

Number right: _____

Unit Four: Language Usage

Name _____ Date _____

Lesson 6: Using degrees of comparison
Part one

DIRECTIONS ▶ Darken the circle of the choice that uses the correct form of the adjective to complete each sentence.

STRATEGY TIPS

1. As you read each sentence, think about the three comparative forms of adjectives and adverbs.
2. The positive degree is used when only one thing is described.
3. The comparative degree is used when two things are compared.
4. The superlative degree is used when three or more things are compared.

Sample:
Of all the final exams I took last week, math was the _____.

Ⓐ easier Ⓒ easiest
Ⓑ most easy Ⓓ more easier

ANSWER

The correct answer is *C easiest*. The math test is being compared to all of the other tests that were taken last week.

NOW TRY THESE

1. Who was the _____ player on the team?
   Ⓐ most best Ⓒ bestest
   Ⓑ more best Ⓓ best

2. Our team is _____ in the standings than any other team in the league.
   Ⓐ higher Ⓒ high
   Ⓑ highest Ⓓ more high

3. Of all the dogs we've owned, Ginger was the _____ to train.
   Ⓐ easier Ⓒ easiest
   Ⓑ most easier Ⓓ more easier

4. The instructions for driving to the park were really _____.
   Ⓐ clear Ⓒ clearest
   Ⓑ clearer Ⓓ more clearer

5. Flying is the _____ way to travel from city to city.
   Ⓐ more most expensive
   Ⓑ expensivest
   Ⓒ most expensivest
   Ⓓ most expensive

6. Our class arrived _____ than the other classes because our bus broke down.
   Ⓐ latest Ⓒ more later
   Ⓑ later Ⓓ late

7. Jodi is the _____ person I know.
   Ⓐ cheerfulest Ⓒ more cheerful
   Ⓑ most cheerful Ⓓ cheerfuler

8. That was the _____ movie I ever saw.
   Ⓐ funnier Ⓒ most funny
   Ⓑ funnest Ⓓ funniest

GO ON TO NEXT PAGE ▶

Name_____   Date _____

Unit Four: Language Usage

Part two

DIRECTIONS ▶ Darken the circle for the correct answer to the questions about degrees of comparison.

NOW TRY THESE

9. Which word in the sentence is a comparative adverb?
   Yesterday I finished my homework earlier than my sister did.
   Ⓐ finished   Ⓑ earlier   Ⓒ than   Ⓓ did

10. Which word in the sentence is a positive adjective?
    I think that Scott is a very nice person.
    Ⓐ very   Ⓑ that   Ⓒ person   Ⓓ nice

11. Which word in the sentence is a comparative adjective?
    That elephant's name is Jumbo because he is larger than the other elephants.
    Ⓐ larger   Ⓑ elephant   Ⓒ name   Ⓓ other

12. Which word in the sentence is a superlative adjective?
    A low-fat diet is the healthiest way to eat.
    Ⓐ diet   Ⓑ low-fat   Ⓒ healthiest   Ⓓ way

13. Which word in the sentence is a superlative adverb?
    We wanted to see who could throw a ball the farthest from the marker.
    Ⓐ wanted   Ⓑ farthest   Ⓒ from   Ⓓ throw

14. Which word in the sentence is a comparative adverb?
    Florrie is less able to sing than Jose because she has a sore throat.
    Ⓐ less   Ⓑ than   Ⓒ able   Ⓓ sore

15. Which word in the sentence is a positive adverb?
    You will know the answer to your question soon.
    Ⓐ know   Ⓑ soon   Ⓒ your   Ⓓ answer

STOP

Your time: _____
Number right: _____

On this lesson I did _____ because _____.

© Steck-Vaughn Company

Unit Four: Language Usage

Name _____ Date _____

Lesson 7: Identifying interjections

DIRECTIONS ▶ Darken the circle for the correct use of an interjection in each of the sentences.

STRATEGY TIPS

1. Remember that interjections are words used to express feeling.
2. Use an exclamation point to show a strong interjection. Start the next sentence with a capital letter.
3. Use a comma after a mild interjection.

Sample:

Which sentence is punctuated correctly?

- Ⓐ Help, I can't hold on any longer.
- Ⓑ Help. I can't hold on any longer.
- Ⓒ Help! I can't hold on any longer.
- Ⓓ Help I can't hold on any longer!

ANSWER

The correct answer is *C Help! I can't hold on any longer.* The exclamation point after the word *help* shows strong feeling.

NOW TRY THESE

1.
   - Ⓐ Wow that was a great show?
   - Ⓑ Wow. That was a great show!
   - Ⓒ Wow, that was a great show!
   - Ⓓ Wow! That was a great show.

2.
   - Ⓐ Oh! Now I get it.
   - Ⓑ Oh, now I get it.
   - Ⓒ Oh, Now I get it
   - Ⓓ Oh. Now I get it!

3.
   - Ⓐ Gosh, I'm glad you can join us.
   - Ⓑ Gosh I'm glad you can join us!
   - Ⓒ Gosh! I'm glad you can join us.
   - Ⓓ Gosh I'm glad you can join us.

4.
   - Ⓐ Ouch, that really hurts.
   - Ⓑ Ouch! That really hurts.
   - Ⓒ Ouch that really hurts
   - Ⓓ Ouch! that really hurts.

5.
   - Ⓐ Well! Let's just try it.
   - Ⓑ Well, Let's just try it.
   - Ⓒ Well, let's just try it.
   - Ⓓ Well, let's just try it!

6.
   - Ⓐ Hurray, we're going to the zoo.
   - Ⓑ Hurray We're going to the zoo.
   - Ⓒ Hurray, We're going to the zoo.
   - Ⓓ Hurray! We're going to the zoo.

STOP

Your time: _____

Number right: _____

On this lesson I did _____ because _____

_____ .

Test Four: Language Usage

Name _____ Date _____

PRACTICE TEST 4
Part 1

Directions: For questions 1-3, darken the circle on your answer sheet for the letter of the correctly spelled word that fits in the blank.

Sample: We're leaving for vacation next ____.

    A Wendsday   **C** Wednesday
    B Wensday   **D** Wedensday

Answer: The correct answer is *C Wednesday*.

1. Our _____ has a great collection of reference books.
   A libary   **B** library   **C** liberry   **D** libreery

2. Frank's grandfather will be ____ years old next month.
   A ninty   **B** nintey   **C** nintie   **D** ninety

3. Have you ever visited a _____ country?
   A foreign   **B** foriegn   **C** forign   **D** foregn

Directions: For questions 4-8, darken the circle on your answer sheet for the letter of the misspelled word.

Sample: **A** definitely   **B** describe   **C** discribe   **D** toward

Answer: The correct answer is *C discribe*.

4.	**A** eighth	**B** grammer	**C** possess	**D** fourth
5.	**A** truly	**B** neighbor	**C** surprise	**D** writen
6.	**A** studying	**B** license	**C** recieve	**D** village
7.	**A** fourty	**B** using	**C** author	**D** across
8.	**A** until	**B** embarras	**C** separate	**D** apology

Test Four: Language Usage

Name _____   Date _____

Part 2

Directions: For questions 9-12, darken the circle on your answer sheet for the letter of the sentence part that should have a capital. Darken *E none* if no capital letter is needed.

Sample: <u>English and french</u>   <u>are the</u>   <u>official Canadian</u>   <u>languages.</u>
            A   B   C   D   E none

Answer: The correct answer is *A English and french*.

9. <u>Most movies</u> <u>are made</u> <u>in</u> <u>hollywood, California.</u>
    A   B   C   D   E none

10. <u>Washington, d. c.</u> <u>is the</u> <u>capital of</u> <u>the United States.</u>
     A   B   C   D   E none

11. <u>My younger brother</u> <u>loved the</u> <u>movie</u> <u>"Home Alone."</u>
        A   B   C   D   E none

12. <u>My mother</u> <u>said to</u> <u>the painters,</u> <u>"please be careful."</u>
     A   B   C   D   E none

Directions: For questions 13-16, darken the circle on your answer sheet for the letter of the punctuation mark that is needed. Darken *E none* if no other mark is needed.

Sample: Mr Denton's store is on Main St. in New Bedford.
       A ,   B .   C "   D ;   E none

Answer: The correct answer is *B*. The abbreviation *Mr.* requires a period.

13. March 21 is the first day of spring.
    A !   B ?   C ;   D "   E none

14. Lavinia wants to go shopping but Joan prefers to go for a walk.
    A ,   B ;   C .   D !   E none

15. Next year I will take science, math, history and Latin.
    A ?   B !   C ,   D ;   E none

16. That is the worst book I ever read
    A ?   B :   C !   D ,   E none

GO ON TO NEXT PAGE

Part 3

Directions: Read the sentences in the article, then darken the circle for the correct answers to questions 17-19. Use your answer sheet to record your answers.

Sample: Which sentence does not belong in the paragraph?
People who were born under the sign of Aries the Ram were born between
(1)
March 21 and April 20. They like to keep fit physically.
  (2)
Arians make good friends. St. Patrick's day is also in March.
         (3)   (4)

    A 4   **B** 3   **C** 2   **D** 1

Answer: The correct answer is *A 4*.

Computers have changed our lives forever. In less than a second, they can do
            (1)   (2)
work that used to take hours, days, or weeks. Suddenly everyone seems to be
                                                                    (3)
"surfing the net." Because the Internet can connect to information
       (4)
and many activities. Just go to any computer store, and you'll see many
                               (5)
people buying computer software. Today more and more families have
                                         (6)
computers in their homes. They wonder how they ever got along
without them.   (7)

17. What is the topic sentence of this paragraph?
    A 6   **B** 7   **C** 4   **D** 1

18. Which is a sentence fragment?
    A 3   **B** 4   **C** 2   **D** 5

19. Which sentence does not belong in the paragraph?
    A 7   **B** 5   **C** 6   **D** 3

Test Four: Language Usage

Name_____ Date_____

Part 4

Directions: For questions 20-22, darken the circle on your answer sheet for the word or words that show the complete subject or complete predicate of each sentence.

Sample: The school orchestra gave a concert.

S1 Which is the complete subject?

A The school
B school orchestra
C a concert
D The school orchestra

S2 Which is the complete predicate?

A gave a concert
B orchestra gave
C The school
D a concert

Answer: The correct answer to S1 is *D The school orchestra*. The correct answer to S2 is *A gave a concert*.

20. Which is the complete subject of this sentence?
    Mr. Bruno showed us how to use his camera.

    A his camera
    B Mr. Bruno
    C how to use
    D to use his camera

21. Which is the complete predicate of this sentence?
    Freda likes to read mystery stories.

    A Freda likes
    B likes to read mystery stories
    C mystery stories
    D read mystery stories

22. Which is the complete predicate of this sentence?
    Jason asked the tour guide a question.

    A asked the tour guide a question
    B Jason asked
    C guide a question
    D tour guide

Part 5

Directions: For questions 23-24, choose the correct pronoun and darken its letter on your answer sheet.

Sample: She hung ____ coat in the closet.
   A you're   B them   C your   D our

Answer: The correct answer is *C your*.

23. It was ____ who ate the cookies.

    A he
    B him
    C her
    D them

24. We applauded ____ acting in the class play.

    A there
    B their
    C they're
    D them

GO ON TO NEXT PAGE

© Steck-Vaughn Company   48   Test Taking 6, SV 6774-3

Name_____ Date_____

Directions: For questions 25-27, choose the pronoun that can replace the underlined words. Darken the letter on your answer sheet.

25. Please tell **Carlos and Cynthia** how to get to the ball game.
    A they   B them   C us   D we

26. Don't forget to return **Martha's** suitcase.
    A her   B our   C she's   D their

27. I'm taking piano lessons, and I'm really enjoying **the lessons**.
    A those   B these   C them   D they

Part 6

Directions: For questions 28-29, mark the letter on your answer sheet for the correct form of the adjective that completes each sentence.

Sample: Serena's handwriting is _____ than her sister's.
    A clearest   B clearer   C most clear   D clear

Answer: The correct answer is *B clearer*.

28. My mother bought me the _____ sweater I ever saw.
    A more beautiful   C most beautiful
    B beautifulest   D most beautifulest

29. Rex is the _____ of all the dogs on our street.
    A fiercer   B fiercest   C fierce   D most fiercest

Part 7

Directions: For questions 30-31, darken the circle on your answer sheet for the correct answer.

Sample: Which sentence is punctuated correctly?
    A Alas! It's raining again, so we can't go   C Alas it's raining again so, we can't go.
    B Alas, it's raining again, so we can't go.   D Alas it's raining again so we can't go!

Answer: The correct answer is *B Alas, it's raining again, so we can't go.*

30. A Help, I can't get down.
    B Help, I can't get down!
    C Help! I can't get down.
    D Help I can't get down.

31. A Aha, now I can see you.
    B Aha! Now I can see you.
    C Aha, Now I can see you.
    D Aha now I can see you!

Suggested Time Limit: 27 minutes   Your time: _____
Check your work if you have time. Wait for instructions from your teacher.

Name_____   Date _____

UNIT V: STUDY SKILLS

Lesson 1: Outlining

DIRECTIONS ▸ Darken the circle for the detail that best completes the outline.

STRATEGY TIPS

1. Remember that an outline is a way of organizing notes to be used when writing reports and compositions.
2. Outlines show main ideas and their supporting details.

Sample:

Kinds of Computers
  I. *Where special purpose computers are used*
    A. *Hotels and restaurants*
    B. _____
    C. *Factories*

  II. *Where general purpose computers are used*
    A. *Homes*
    B. *Offices*
    C. _____

Which detail fits in line II–C ?

  Ⓐ Elections   Ⓒ Supermarkets
  Ⓑ Schools   Ⓓ Department stores

ANSWER
The correct answer is *B Schools*. The other choices are about special purposes.

NOW TRY THESE

About Eyes
  I. *Parts of the eye*
    A. *Iris*
    B. *Cornea*
    C. _____

  II. *How the eye works*
    A. *Focusing*
    B. *Depth perception*
    C. *Effects of light on the eye*

  III. *Vision problems*
    A. _____
    B. *Nearsightedness*
    C. *Astigmatism*
    D. *Color blindness*

1. Which detail fits line I–C?
  Ⓐ Eyeglasses   Ⓒ Eyebrows
  Ⓑ Lens   Ⓓ Eye banks

2. Which detail fits in line III–A?
  Ⓐ Lens   Ⓒ Farsightedness
  Ⓑ Tears   Ⓓ Light rays

GO ON TO NEXT PAGE

Name_____ Date _____

Unit Five: Study Skills

Wildflowers

I. Common names
   A. Goldthread
   B. Cloudberry
   C. Blue flag

II. _____
   A. Iris versicolor
   B. Coptis trifola
   C. Rubus Chamaemorus

III. Habitat
   A. Seashore
   B. _____
   C. Woodlands

3. Which is the main idea topic for line II?
   Ⓐ Florists   Ⓒ Trees
   Ⓑ Garden flowers   Ⓓ Latin names

4. Which detail belongs in line III–B?
   Ⓐ Roadsides   Ⓒ Florists
   Ⓑ Nurseries   Ⓓ Greenhouses

Popular Sports

I. Sports you can play alone
   A. Bowling
   B. _____
   C. Canoeing
   D. Skiing

II. _____
   A. Basketball
   B. Baseball
   C. _____
   D. Soccer

5. Which detail best fits line I–B?
   Ⓐ Boxing   Ⓒ Hockey
   Ⓑ Swimming   Ⓓ Relay racing

6. Which topic fits line II ?
   Ⓐ Indoor sports   Ⓒ Team sports
   Ⓑ Winter sports   Ⓓ Summer sports

7. Which detail fits line II–C?
   Ⓐ Horseback riding   Ⓒ Hiking
   Ⓑ Golf   Ⓓ Football

STOP

Your time: _____

Number right: _____

On this lesson I did _____ because _____

_____.

I think it would help me to _____

_____.

Name_____ Date _____

Unit Five: Study Skills

Lesson 2: Understanding visual information

DIRECTIONS ▶ Darken the circle for the correct answer.

STRATEGY TIPS

1. Read the title to understand what the information is about.
2. Always study the legend or key before reading a map, chart, or graph.

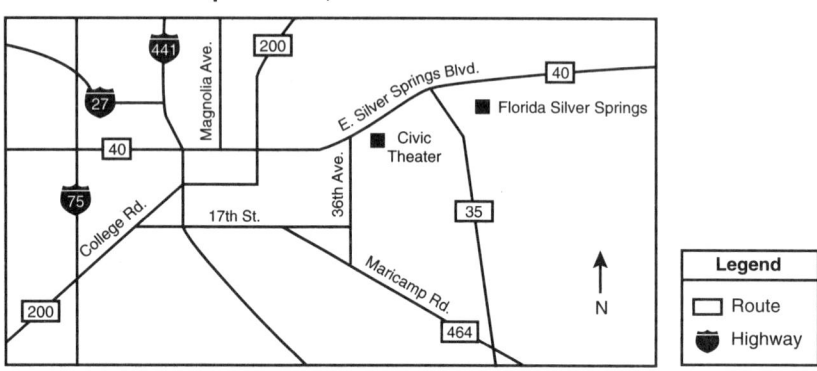

Sample:

What is the name of the road on route 464?

Ⓐ Collins   Ⓒ Maricamp
Ⓑ E. Silver Springs   Ⓓ Magnolia

ANSWER

The correct answer is *C Maricamp*.

NOW TRY THESE

1. On which route is the Civic Theater located?

   Ⓐ Route 40   Ⓒ Route 200
   Ⓑ Route 35   Ⓓ Route 75

2. Which direction should you travel on Route 40 to get to Florida Silver Springs from Civic Theater?

   Ⓐ southwest   Ⓒ northwest
   Ⓑ southeast   Ⓓ northeast

3. What is the number of the major highway that Route 40 crosses?

   Ⓐ 441   Ⓒ 27
   Ⓑ 75   Ⓓ 35

Name_____   Date _____

Unit V, lesson 2, page 2

National Parks in Alaska		
Park	Date Founded	Area in Acres
Denali	1917	4,065,493
Gates of the Arctic	1980	7,052,000
Glacier Bay	1980	3,878,269
Kalmal	1980	4,430,125
Kobuk Valley	1980	1,710,000
Wrangell-St. Elias	1980	8,147,000

4. Which is the oldest national park in Alaska?
   - Ⓐ Glacier Bay
   - Ⓑ Kobuk Valley
   - Ⓒ Kalmal
   - Ⓓ Denali

5. Which park has the greatest number of acres?
   - Ⓐ Kalmal
   - Ⓑ Wrangell-St. Elias
   - Ⓒ Gates of the Arctic
   - Ⓓ Kobuk Valley

Map of Orwell River Tributary

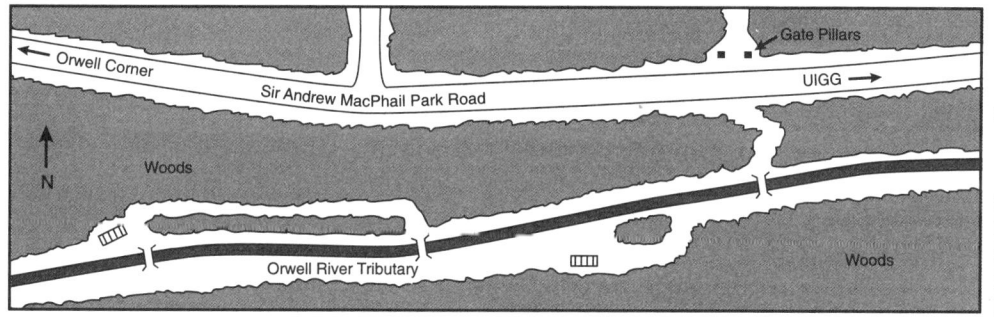

6. How many feet does each quarter inch on the scale represent?
   - Ⓐ 10
   - Ⓑ 5
   - Ⓒ 50
   - Ⓓ 100

7. How many walking bridges go across the Orwell River Tributary?
   - Ⓐ Two
   - Ⓑ Three
   - Ⓒ Four
   - Ⓓ None

8. Where will you find a rest area?
   - Ⓐ gate pillars
   - Ⓑ woods
   - Ⓒ Orwell River Tributary
   - Ⓓ UIGG

Your time:_____

Number right:_____

Name_____   Date _____

Unit Five: Study Skills

Lesson 3: Using an index

DIRECTIONS ▶ Study the index below. Darken the circle for the correct answer.

 **STRATEGY TIPS**

1. Remember that an index lists each section or topic in alphabetical order.
2. All the pages that deal with a particular topic can be found in the index.

INDEX

Adirondacks, 39, 137
Alaska, 12, 57, 173
Alps, climbing peaks of, 158-160,
    farming in, 20-21

Birds, 39, 108, 114-115

Cable cars, 23
Canadian Rockies, 48, 130
Colorado Rockies, vegetation of, 83-86, 90

Dairy farming, 21-27
Deer, 109
Douglas fir, 83

Eagle, 114
Earth core, 34, 35, 36, 58

Field, Darby, 158
Flies, 116
Flowers, alpine, 84-85, 86-87, 89

Sample:
How many pages in this book have information on Alaska?

ⓐ five   ⓒ six
ⓑ three   ⓓ one

ANSWER
The correct answer is *B three*. The index tells you that information about Alaska will be found on pages 12, 57, and 173.

NOW TRY THESE

1. Where will you find information about mountain climbing in the Alps?

    ⓐ 20-21   ⓒ 114-115
    ⓑ 48   ⓓ 158-160

2. What kind of flowers are described on pages 86-87?

    ⓐ mountain flowers ⓒ alpine flowers
    ⓑ wildflowers   ⓓ tropical flowers

3. How many pages have information about the Canadian Rockies?

    ⓐ one   ⓒ forty
    ⓑ two   ⓓ eighty-two

4. If you look on page 83, you will find information about ___.

    ⓐ flies   ⓒ eagles
    ⓑ Douglas fir   ⓓ deer

5. If you read page 173, you will find information about ___.

    ⓐ Alaska   ⓒ Colorado Rockies
    ⓑ Darby Field   ⓓ Earth core

6. What kind of bird will you read about on page 114?

    ⓐ alpine   ⓒ all kinds
    ⓑ eagle   ⓓ cable

STOP

Your time:_____   Number right:_____

Unit Five: Study Skills

Name_____ Date _____

Lesson 4: Using a table of contents

DIRECTIONS ▶ Study the table of contents below. Then darken the circle for the correct answer.

 **STRATEGY TIPS**

1. Remember that a table of contents lists each section or topic in the book in the order in which it appears.
2. Read straight across the line to find the beginning page number of a chapter.

CONTENTS
Unit 1: Exploring Ideas
    SKILLS LESSON: Your Reading Vocabulary 4
      This Man Was Mother to a Duck by Helen Kay 16
      Breaking the Bee's Code by Millicent E. Selsam 22
      The Story of Weights and Measures by Jeanne Bendick 27
      Margaret Mead in Samoa by Dorothy Nathan 33
    TEXTBOOK STUDY: Building Vocabulary..............42
Unit 2: People of the Past
    SKILLS LESSON: Meaning in Sentences 50
      Men of the Nile Valley by Enid I. Meadowcroft..........58
      Sea-Rovers of the North by Louise Dickinson Rich 64
      The Tournament by Sean Morrison 71
      Marco Polo's Great Adventure by Roger Duvoisin 79
    TEXTBOOK STUDY: Understanding Sentences 89

Sample:
On which page would you read about Understanding Sentences?

Ⓐ page 50   Ⓒ page 42
Ⓑ page 89   Ⓓ page 79

ANSWER: The correct answer is *B page 89.*

NOW TRY THESE

1. On which page does Millicent E. Selsam's story about bees start?

   Ⓐ page 16   Ⓒ page 22
   Ⓑ page 27   Ⓓ page 42

2. On which page does Building Vocabulary start?

   Ⓐ page 4   Ⓒ page 33
   Ⓑ page 42   Ⓓ page 89

3. Who wrote *The Story of Weights and Measures*?

   Ⓐ Margaret Mead   Ⓒ Jeanne Bendick
   Ⓑ Dorothy Nathan   Ⓓ Helen Kay

4. On which page does the story about Marco Polo start?

   Ⓐ page 79   Ⓒ page 33
   Ⓑ page 89   Ⓓ page 64

STOP

Your time:_____

Number right:_____

© Steck-Vaughn Company   Test Taking 6, SV 6774-3

Name_____ Date_____

Lesson 5: Using dictionary skills
Part one

DIRECTIONS ▶ Darken the circle for the correct answer.

STRATEGY TIPS

1. Look carefully at each pair of guide words. They tell you the first and last words on a dictionary page.
2. Remember that entry words are always in alphabetical order.

Sample:
Which entry word belongs between the guide words **ranger/ratio**?

Ⓐ range
Ⓑ raise
Ⓒ rasp
Ⓓ rattan

ANSWER

The correct answer is *C rasp*. *Range* and *raise* come before *ranger*. *Rattan* comes after *ratio*.

NOW TRY THESE

1. Which entry word would not fit between **fertilizer** and **fiftieth**?

    Ⓐ few
    Ⓑ file
    Ⓒ fiction
    Ⓓ feud

2. On which guide word page would you find the entry word **mice**?

    Ⓐ message/microphone
    Ⓑ microscope/military
    Ⓒ milk/mine
    Ⓓ microbe/mile

3. Which of these words would be found on a dictionary page between the guide words **devout/diction**?

    Ⓐ devise
    Ⓑ devote
    Ⓒ diet
    Ⓓ diary

4. Which entry word would not fit between **typify** and **unbecoming**?

    Ⓐ umpire
    Ⓑ uncle
    Ⓒ typist
    Ⓓ ugly

5. Which entry word would fit between the guide words **inscribe/instance**?

    Ⓐ instead
    Ⓑ insert
    Ⓒ instant
    Ⓓ insure

6. Which entry word would fit between the guide words **eyelash/faint**?

    Ⓐ fable
    Ⓑ eyebrow
    Ⓒ exult
    Ⓓ fair

GO ON TO NEXT PAGE

Name_____   Date _____

Part two

DIRECTIONS ▶ For questions 7-10, use the dictionary entries below to answer the questions.

STRATEGY TIPS

1. Many words have more than one meaning. Think about the meaning that best fits the context of the sentence.
2. The same word can be a noun, a verb, or an adjective. Decide which would be correct for the sentence.

bright adj.   **1.** Shedding much light; shining; glowing **2.** Very clear or vivid **3.** Clever **4.** Lively

club n.   **1.** A heavy wooden stick used as a weapon **2.** The stick, bat, or mallet used in striking a ball in various games; as a golf club **3.** A group of people associated for a common purpose **4.** The rooms or building used by a group

double adj.   **1.** Twofold; multiplied by two; being twice as great, as large, as much **2.** Being in pairs **3.** Combining two things, usually unlike — n. **4.** Twice as much, as in number, amount, or value **5.** A person or thing that closely resembles another; a duplicate — v. **6.** To make twice as great; to multiply by two **7.** To duplicate; to be the double of **8.** To make of two thicknesses; to fold; to clench **9.** To go back over the same ground

Sample:
Which definition of **bright** means *someone who is smart*?

Ⓐ Definition 1   Ⓒ Definition 3
Ⓑ Definition 2   Ⓓ Definition 4

ANSWER
The correct answer is *C Definition 3*. A smart person can be clever.

NOW TRY THESE

7. In which of these sentences is definition 4 for the word **club** used correctly?

   Ⓐ My new golf club feels just right.
   Ⓑ We're having dinner at the club tonight.
   Ⓒ The French club meets after school.
   Ⓓ The police officer carried a club.

Darken the circle for the definition that best defines the underlined word.

8. That girl is her sister's <u>double</u>.

   Ⓐ 3   Ⓒ 2
   Ⓑ 5   Ⓓ 6

9. We all enjoyed listening to the <u>bright</u> tunes that the band played.

   Ⓐ 3   Ⓒ 1
   Ⓑ 4   Ⓓ 2

10. Eight is the <u>double</u> of four.

    Ⓐ 2   Ⓒ 8
    Ⓑ 4   Ⓓ 3

Your time:_____
Number right:_____

Test Five: Study Skills

Name_____   Date_____

PRACTICE TEST 5
Part 1

Directions: Look at the outline. For questions 1-3, darken the circle on the answer sheet for the correct answer.

Potatoes
I. Varieties of potatoes
    A. Baking potatoes
    B. All-purpose potatoes
II. _____
    A. Planting potatoes
    B. Harvesting potatoes
III. Using pesticides

Sample: Which of these fits best in line II?

  A Other kinds of potatoes
  B Cooking potatoes
  C Potato recipes
  D Growing potatoes

Answer: The correct answer is *D Growing potatoes.*

Bicycles
I. Early bicycles
    A. Bicycles without pedals
    B. Some names for early bicycles
       1. Hobby horses
       2. _____
II. Late 1800s
    A. 1870, the "ordinary bicycle"
       1. How the high wheeler worked
       2. Problems with the high wheeler
    B. _____
       1. Why people loved the new bicycle
       2. Differences between the safety bicycle and the ordinary bicycle
III. _____
    A. Racing bikes
    B. Mountain bikes
    C. Tandems

1. Which best fits line I-B-2?
  A Horseless carriage
  B Boneshakers
  C Tricycles
  D Gas-savers

2. Which best fits line II-B?
  A Riding bicycles
  B Bicycle races
  C A new kind of bicycle
  D Bicycle uses

3. Which best fits line III?
  A Modern bicycles
  B Bicycle trips
  C Power bikes
  D Bicycle tires

Name_____   Date _____

Part 2

Directions: Study this map of the state of Maine. Then darken the correct circle on the answer sheet to answer questions 4-7.

Sample: What is the name of the lake in Baxter State Park?

 A Western Lakes
 B Katahdin
 C Moosehead Lake
 D Island Falls Lake

Answer: The correct answer is
C Moosehead Lake.

Maine Map

---

4. Heading north on Route 95, which city is between Brunswick and Waterville?

   A Bangor
   B Augusta
   C Portland
   D Bath

5. Acadia National Park is near _____.

   A Greenville
   B Bar Harbor
   C Eastport
   D Machias

6. The northernmost town in Maine is _____.

   A Madawaska
   B Van Buren
   C Caribou
   D Fort Fairfield

7. Maine's southernmost town is _____.

   A Biddeford
   B Stonington
   C Boothbay Harbor
   D Kittery

Directions: Use the chart below to answer questions 8-9. Record your answers on the answer sheet.

Some Important Transportation Dates

1750	First Conestoga wagon is built.
1807	Fulton's steamboat is launched.
1859	The first railroad across the United States is completed.
1903	The Wright brothers fly their airplane.
1908	The Model T Ford is introduced.
1927	Lindbergh makes the first solo nonstop flight across the Atlantic Ocean.
1969	Neil Armstrong is the first person to walk on the moon.

Name_____ Date _____

Practice test 5, part 2, page 2

8. How many dates tell about air transportation?

    A seven
    B three
    C two
    D one

9. Which transportation event made cross-country travel easier?

    A the steamboat
    B the Conestoga wagon
    C the railroad
    D moon landing

Part 3

Directions: Study the index below to answer questions 10-12. Record your answers on the answer sheet.

Application programs 37-42
    forcing to quit or restart 114
    increasing memory for 60
    installing 38
Backing up 40
Basic skills
    with mouse 12-13
    tutorial review 12-13

Definitions of items on screen 13, 16
Dialog boxes 53
Disk drive 78
Eject CD command 45, 67
    ejecting a floppy disk 42
Electromagnetic emissions 87
Files, backing up 40
    floppy disks 93

Sample: On which page will you find out how to eject a floppy disk?

    A page 37   C page 45
    B page 42   D page 67

Answer: The correct answer is *B page 42*.

---

10. Which two pages have definitions?

    A 12, 13   C 37, 42
    B 45, 67   D 13, 16

11. On which page will you find out how to back up a file?

    A page 40   C page 46
    B page 42   D page 93

12. On which page will you find information on installing application programs?

    A page 60   C page 38
    B page 37   D page 42

GO ON TO NEXT PAGE

Test Five: Study Skills

Name _____   Date _____

Part 4

Directions: For questions 13-14, study the table of contents. Then darken the circle on the answer sheet for the correct answer.

Unit 1: Narrative Text
Chapter One: Strategies for Answering Character Questions 6
Chapter Two: Strategies for Answering Story Structure Questions 16
Chapter Three: Strategies for Answering Literary Awareness Questions. 23
Chapter Four: Strategies for Answering Vocabulary Questions 26

13. Which chapter might include this sentence? "A single word can have many meanings."

    A Chapter Five   C Chapter Four
    B Chapter One   D Chapter Two

14. Which chapter might discuss questions about setting, plot, or theme?

    A Chapter Two   C Chapter Four
    B Chapter Three   D Chapter Five

Part 5

Directions: For questions 15-16, study the following dictionary entries. Then darken the circle for the correct answer.

deal v. **1.** To give out in portions or shares; to distribute; as to deal cards **2.** To give or deliver; as to deal someone a blow **3.** To have to do; as a book that deals with space **4.** To treat, act or do **5.** To buy and sell; to trade; to carry on business

late adj. **1.** Coming or doing something after the usual or proper time; tardy **2.** Toward the end or close; as of a day or night **3.** Having recently died or left a certain position **4.** Recent; as in late news—adv. After the usual or proper time

Sample: Which of the definitions of <u>deal</u> means *distributing portions*?

   A Definition 1   C Definition 3   **Answer:** The correct answer is
   B Definition 2   D Definition 4   *A Definition 1.*

15. Which of the following is an example of Definition 4 of the word <u>deal</u>?

    A give out the cards
    B do business
    C treat fairly
    D deliver a surprise

16. Which of the following definitions of <u>late</u> means *someone who is not living*?

    A Definition 1
    B Definition 2
    C Definition 3
    D Definition 4

STOP

Suggested Time Limit: 20 minutes   Your time: _____
Check your work if you have time. Wait for instructions from your teacher.

Name_____   Date _____

UNIT VI: READING COMPREHENSION

Lesson 1: Finding the main idea

DIRECTIONS ▶ Darken the circle for the answer that best expresses the main idea of each selection. Darken *E none* if the correct answer is not given.

STRATEGY TIPS

1. Think about all the details in the selection.
2. Decide what all the details are about. This is the main idea.

Sample:

Horses today look very different than their ancestors. The first horses were not much larger than rabbits. They lived in forests and were called Eohippus, or Dawn Horse, because they lived at the beginning of the Age of Mammals. The Dawn Horse had four toes on each front foot and three toes on each hind foot. Horses today have only one toe on both front and hind legs. The hoof is actually the nail of that toe.

Ⓐ Horses' toes   Ⓓ Horses of the forest
Ⓑ Ancestors of the horse   Ⓔ None
Ⓒ The Age of Mammals

Answer: The correct answer is *B Ancestors of the horse. A, C,* and *D* are mentioned, but they do not tell what the entire selection is about.

NOW TRY THESE

1.   During the 1800s, the number of immigrants to America increased rapidly, from 150,000 during the 1820s, to 1.7 million in the 1840s, and 2.5 million in the 1850s.

   The 1800s are often referred to as the first wave of immigration to the United States. Three catastrophic events were the main reasons behind it: the end of the Napoleonic Wars in 1815, the potato famines of the 1840s in Ireland, and the change in economic conditions in Europe caused by the Industrial Revolution.

Ⓐ Three catastrophic events   Ⓓ Millions of immigrants
Ⓑ The potato famines   Ⓔ None
Ⓒ The Industrial Revolution

Name_____   Date _____

Unit VI, lesson 1, page 2

2.   From the earliest colonial days, regulation and inspection of immigrants were the responsibilities of each individual state. The first federal immigration law wasn't enacted until 1819.

   The states' greatest fear was that immigrants would bring the dreaded diseases of smallpox, typhoid fever, and cholera with them. Screening of new immigrants focused almost completely on quarantine. As the immigrants disembarked at a port, a health inspector quickly scanned them for signs of contagious diseases. In New York, immigrants who were thought to have any of these diseases were sent to Marine Hospital on Staten Island.

   - Ⓐ Reasons for screening immigrants
   - Ⓑ Contagious diseases
   - Ⓒ The first federal immigration law
   - Ⓓ Inspection of immigrants
   - Ⓔ None

3.   In prehistoric times, people had only one means of transportation. They walked and had to drag or carry their things with them. About seven thousand years ago, people started using pack animals to carry heavy loads. Although pack animals didn't make traveling faster, they made it easier to move heavy loads.

   Two of the first animals to be used were the donkey and the ox. Other animals were the llama, the elephant, and the camel. Later the horse became a useful pack animal. These animals are still used for transportation in many parts of the world today.

   - Ⓐ Pack animals for transportation
   - Ⓑ Prehistoric times
   - Ⓒ Why people had to walk
   - Ⓓ Making traveling faster
   - Ⓔ None

4.   Some of our former presidents are honored in Washington D.C. George Washington is honored with a tall, white tower of granite called the Washington Monument. Visitors take elevators to the very top. From there they can see a fantastic view of the city. The Lincoln Memorial honors our sixteenth president. Inside is a giant statue of Mr. Lincoln sitting in a big chair. The words of his most famous speech are on the walls. Thomas Jefferson is honored with a monument on the banks of the Potomac River. In 1996 a monument to Franklin D. Roosevelt was unveiled.

   - Ⓐ Our former presidents
   - Ⓑ Granite monuments
   - Ⓒ Honoring some former presidents
   - Ⓓ Fantastic city views
   - Ⓔ None

Your time:_____

Number right:_____

Name_____ Date _____

Lesson 2: Drawing conclusions

DIRECTIONS ▶ Darken the circle for the answer that tells the conclusion that can be drawn after reading the selection. Darken *E none* if there is no correct answer.

STRATEGY TIPS

1. Read the entire selection as though you were looking for clues.
2. What conclusion can you make after thinking about all of the details?

Sample:

After World War I, new immigration laws were passed. In 1917 a law was passed specifying thirty-three classes of foreigners who could not be admitted to the United States. Immigrants who were admitted had to pass a literacy test. This new law greatly reduced the number of immigrants for a while, but by 1921 the number of arrivals again climbed to 500,000. New, stricter laws were enacted in 1921 and again in 1924. Organizations like the Immigration Restriction League and labor groups supported these laws.

What conclusion can you draw from this paragraph?

- Ⓐ Literacy tests are important.
- Ⓑ There are many classes of foreigners.
- Ⓒ We need new stricter laws.
- Ⓓ Some organizations wanted to reduce the number of immigrants.
- Ⓔ None

Answer: The correct answer is *D Some organizations wanted to reduce the number of immigrants*. None of the other statements are conclusions that can be drawn from this paragraph.

NOW TRY THESE

1. Before railroads or automobiles, carriages were used to transport people. They were similar to cars, but they didn't have motors. Carriages were pulled by horses, donkeys, or mules.

   During the Middle Ages in Europe, carriages were not used very often. The roads were unpaved and usually in very poor condition. Carriages gained popularity once new roads were built. During their time, carriages provided useful and convenient transportation.

   - Ⓐ Carriages don't have motors.
   - Ⓑ Good roads were important for carriage travel.
   - Ⓒ Carriage transportation is popular.
   - Ⓓ There are many unpaved roads.
   - Ⓔ None

Name _____   Date _____

Unit VI, lesson 2, page 2

2.   At one time, people in the United States got most of the things they needed from within the country. Oranges came from Florida, Texas, or California. Lumber came from Oregon. Most clocks, watches, and shoes came from the New England states. Automobiles came from Detroit, Michigan.

   Today we get food and supplies from all over the world. Cars can come from Japan. We import shoes from Brazil, Korea, and China. Many of the clothes we wear are made in the Far East or Balkan countries.

   Ⓐ Shoes are manufactured in New England.
   Ⓑ Japanese cars are very good.
   Ⓒ We get things we need from all over the world.
   Ⓓ We need oranges.
   Ⓔ None

3.   Thousands of years ago, the native people of India far outnumbered their conquerors. In order to keep control over the native people, the conquerors invented a plan called the caste system. The conquerors belonged to the highest class. The natives belonged to the lower classes.

   There were special rules which had to be followed. No person of one caste could eat with a member of another caste. No one could marry into another caste. Any one who broke the rules was severely punished. The caste system in India was practiced by Hindus. Most high-caste Hindus thought that they couldn't come near the lowest caste, who were known as untouchables. They thought it would make them impure.

   Ⓐ Native Indians liked the caste system.
   Ⓑ The caste system kept people down.
   Ⓒ Caste system rules are fair.
   Ⓓ It is easy to conquer other people.
   Ⓔ None

Your time: _____

Number right: _____

On this lesson I did _____ because _____.

I think it would help me to _____

_____.

Name_____   Date _____

Lesson 3: Recognizing cause and effect

DIRECTIONS ▶ Darken the circle for the answer that shows the cause or effect of something described in the selections below.

STRATEGY TIPS

1. Remember that cause and effect statements are usually related to main ideas and supporting details.
2. Look for signal words, such as *because, since, until, unless, after.*

Sample:

Before the War of 1812, British ships often stopped and searched American ships. They were looking for English soldiers who had left England without permission. This action made Americans angry. President Thomas Jefferson requested that Congress declare an embargo. This meant that American ships could not leave American ports, nor could any foreign ships enter our ports. The idea was to keep England and France from getting badly needed American goods. When it became obvious that Americans were getting hurt by the embargo, Jefferson lifted it.

S1 What was the cause of the embargo?

Ⓐ The British needed our goods.
Ⓑ The British searched American ships.
Ⓒ Jefferson asked Congress to declare an embargo.
Ⓓ Jefferson lifted the embargo.

S2 What was one effect of the embargo?

Ⓐ England and France needed our goods.
Ⓑ English soldiers left England.
Ⓒ American ships couldn't leave our ports.
Ⓓ The War of 1812 stopped.

Answer: **S1** The answer is *B The British searched American ships.*
S2 The answer is *C American ships couldn't leave our ports.*

NOW TRY THESE

Sometimes people aren't able to watch their favorite TV programs because they aren't on at a convenient time. Modern technology has now made it easy for people to watch their favorite programs no matter what time they are on TV. With VCRs people can tape a program and watch it at another time.

1. What is the cause of people using VCRs?

Ⓐ Programs aren't very good.
Ⓑ Modern technology is convenient.
Ⓒ TV programs don't come on at convenient times.
Ⓓ They can't watch TV programs.

Unit VI, lesson 3, page 2

2. What is the effect of having a VCR?

   Ⓐ Modern technology makes things easy.
   Ⓑ People can tape programs to watch at another time.
   Ⓒ TV programs have become better.
   Ⓓ People have favorite TV programs.

   When Paul scored the winning goal for his hockey team, a huge cheer went up from his happy teammates. This was the first time that they beat Bluefield High. Paul was named Most Valuable Player.

3. What was the cause of the huge cheer?

   Ⓐ Paul scored the winning goal.
   Ⓑ The team lost to Bluefield High.
   Ⓒ Paul's teammates were happy.
   Ⓓ Paul was named Most Valuable Player.

4. What was the effect of Paul scoring the winning goal?

   Ⓐ The team got new uniforms.
   Ⓑ Bluefield High students were happy.
   Ⓒ Paul was named Most Valuable Player.
   Ⓓ Bluefield High students let out a huge cheer.

STOP

Your time: _____
Number right: _____

On this lesson I did _____ because _____

_____.

I think it would help me to _____ _____

_____

_____.

Name_____   Date _____

Lesson 4: Recognizing fact and opinion

DIRECTIONS ▶ Darken the circle for the correct answer about facts and opinions.

STRATEGY TIPS
1. Remember that a fact must be provable.
2. Words like *should/would, most/many, everyone knows* are usually used to express opinions.

Sample:

Today, with more than 20 million people, Mexico City is the largest metropolis in the world. Despite its modernization, the city's rich and colorful history is still alive. From its architecture to its culture and its food, many people agree that Mexico City is a fascinating city to visit.

Which statement is a fact?

- Ⓐ Mexico City is fascinating.
- Ⓑ Mexico City has colorful food.
- Ⓒ Mexico City is the largest metropolis in the world.
- Ⓓ Mexico City is very modern.

Answer: The correct answer is *C Mexico City is the largest metropolis in the world*. This is a fact that can be proved. The other answers are opinions.

NOW TRY THESE

1. Virginia City, Nevada, is a great place to visit. Although it is a ghost town today, it was once the richest mining town in the world. Money from its mines financed both the building of San Francisco and the Civil War. In its heyday, it had more than 30,000 residents. When fire destroyed more than 2,000 structures in 1875, the town rebuilt in a year. It is now a national landmark and looks much the way it did.

   Which statement is an opinion?

   - Ⓐ Virginia City was once the richest mining town in the world.
   - Ⓑ There was a fire in Virginia City in 1875.
   - Ⓒ It took only one year to rebuild the city.
   - Ⓓ Virginia City is a great place to visit.

GO ON TO NEXT PAGE ▶

Name_____   Date _____

Unit VI, lesson 4, page 2

2. One of the most popular tourist attractions in Florida is Disney World. Children love to go there. It is located in Orlando. Mickey Mouse, Donald Duck, and other Disney characters can be seen there.

    Which statement is a fact?

    Ⓐ Children love to go to Disney World.
    Ⓑ Disney World is one of the most popular attractions in Florida.
    Ⓒ Everyone loves Mickey Mouse.
    Ⓓ Disney characters make everyone happy.

3. Even though it is not the largest section of the country, the Northeast has the greatest number of people. In fact, the Northeast only makes up about one twentieth of the total land mass of the United States. However, one fourth of all Americans live there. Most people prefer to live in the Northeast because some of our nation's largest cities are located in this part of the country.

    Which statement is an opinion?

    Ⓐ Most people prefer to live in the Northeast.
    Ⓑ One fourth of all Americans live in the Northeast.
    Ⓒ The Northeast is not the largest section of our country.
    Ⓓ The Northeast makes up one twentieth of the total United States land mass.

4. Most states now have recycling programs. However, they all need to expand what is being recycled. Most towns recycle cans, glass, paper, cardboard, and magazines. Yet we still buy many items made of plastic and foam. Currently only about 5% of these materials are recycled. If we want to reduce the amount of garbage we throw away, we must make changes in the way we do recycling.

    Which statement is a fact?

    Ⓐ Every state should have a recycling program.
    Ⓑ Plastic and foam items are easy to recycle.
    Ⓒ Only about 5% of foam and plastic materials is being recycled.
    Ⓓ Most towns now recycle glass and cans.

STOP

Your time: _____
Number right: _____

On this lesson I did _____ because _____

Name_____   Date_____

PRACTICE TEST 6
Part 1

Directions: For question 1, darken the circle on the answer sheet for the statement that expresses the main idea of the paragraph. Darken *E none* if the correct answer is <u>not given</u>.

Sample:
America probably could not have won its freedom from the British during the American Revolution without the help of the French. France provided arms, ships, money, and men to the American colonies. Some Frenchmen even became high-ranking officers in the American army. One of these men was the Marquis de Lafayette, a close friend of George Washington's.

What is the main idea of this paragraph?
A George Washington's friend
B The American colonies
C How the French helped the Americans
D The American Revolution
E none

Answer: The correct answer is *C How the French helped the Americans.*

---

1. What is the main idea of the following selection?

   Frédéric-Auguste Bartholdi, the sculptor who designed the Statue of Liberty, began his career as a painter. He was 18 when he received his first commission for a public monument. The statue he designed was 12 feet tall. It was moved out of his studio with only one inch to spare. That statue established his reputation as a sculptor. It led to more commissions for oversized patriotic works.

   A Bartholdi was a good painter.
   B Only young men can do large sculptures.
   C Bartholdi was always famous.
   D Bartholdi created many huge sculptures.
   E None

Test Six: Reading Comprehension

Name_____ Date_____

Part 2

Directions: For question 2, darken the circle for the answer that tells the conclusion that can be drawn after reading the selection. Darken *E none* if there is no correct answer.

Sample:

Whales are found in all the oceans of the world. Some whales live in very deep water, so they are rarely seen. Other whales live near the shore where they can be seen often. Whales travel from place to place during different times of the year. Part of the year they feed in the cold waters near the North and South Poles. Whales travel to warmer waters to have their babies.

It can be concluded that _____.

A Whales are hard to find.
B Some whales are shy.
C All whales prefer deep water.
D Whales like to travel.
E None

Answer: The correct answer is *E none*.

---

2. The moon is smaller than Earth. It is about 238,000 miles away from Earth. The moon has no air. During the day, the moon is unbearably hot. At night it is colder than the North Pole. The moon is covered with dusty flat land and has many craters.

On July 20, 1969, Neil Armstrong made history by being the first man to walk on the moon. He had to wear a special space suit to protect himself from the moon's environment. Armstrong and other astronauts helped us learn a lot about the moon.

It can be concluded that _____.

A You cannot live on the moon.
B July 20 is a holiday.
C Space travel is exciting.
D It is always cold on the moon.
E None

Test Six: Reading Comprehension

Name_____ Date_____

Part 3

Directions: For questions 3-4, darken the circle on the answer sheet for the answer that shows the cause or effect of something described in the selection below.

Sample:

Henry Ford introduced the Model T in 1908. The design remained the same for many years. In 1913 Ford started making the Model T in a factory using an assembly line. Making lots of cars exactly the same brought down the cost of manufacturing them. By 1925 the price was down from $850 to just $260. At that price, you didn't have to be rich to buy a car.

S1   What was the cause of the lower-priced cars?

   A the Model T   **C** rich people
   B assembly line production **D** the same design

S2   What was the effect of the lower prices?

   A Designs could change.   **C** More people could buy cars.
   B Factories were started. **D** The price went down to $260.

Answer: The correct answer to **S1** is *B assembly line production*. The correct answer to **S2** is *C More people could buy cars*.

Most of the country of Norway is very close to the ocean. Therefore, fishing is an important industry. Fleets of ships leave from different port cities each day. These ships do not use rods to catch the great variety of marine life found in Norway's waters. They use nets. First, the sailors lay out their nets. They mark each location and then go on to lay others. When they return and lift their nets into the boats, they find many kinds of fish in the nets.

3. What is the effect of Norway's location near the ocean?

   A There are lots of beaches.   **C** Many sailors use nets
   B Fishing is a major industry.   **D** Sailors lay out nets.

4. What is the cause of Norway's fishing industry?

   A They don't use rods to catch fish. **C** It is close to the ocean.
   B Ships leave port cities.   **D** Many fish are caught in the nets.

Name_____   Date _____

Part 4

Directions: For question 5, darken the circle on the answer sheet for the correct answer about facts and opinions.

Sample:

   The Oregon Trail was the land route used by many pioneers to settle the Pacific Northwest. The most common form of travel was by Conestoga wagon. Travel on the trail was dangerous. These brave pioneers had to cross swollen rivers and deal with disease, breakdowns, starvation, and lack of water. It was not uncommon to lose a quarter of the people from a wagon train before it reached its destination.

Which is an opinion?

A The rivers were swollen.
B The pioneers were brave.
C There was disease.
D The wagons broke down.

Answer: The correct answer is *B The pioneers were brave.*

   Television programs are more violent than ever. A recent national poll showed that 80% of adults think that there is too much violence on TV. Of these people, 59% say they are personally bothered by violent scenes. Yet, when students were polled, they didn't see anything wrong with the violence.

   Television networks are beginning to recognize the problem. They have been holding meetings to discuss how to reduce TV violence.

5. Which is an opinion?

   A Television is more violent than ever.
   B Students don't see anything wrong.
   C 59% of people polled are bothered by violence.
   D 80% of adults think there is too much violence.

STOP

Suggested Time Limit: 15 minutes   Your time: _____
Check your work if you have time. Wait for instructions from your teacher.

Unit Seven: Math Concepts and Computation

Name_____ Date _____

UNIT VII: MATH CONCEPTS AND COMPUTATION

Lesson 1: Understanding numeration and practicing computation
Part one

DIRECTIONS ▶ Darken the circle for the correct answer.

STRATEGY TIPS

1. Read the question carefully before choosing your answer.
2. Think about the place value of numbers.

Sample:
How would you write the expanded form of 4,018?

Ⓐ 4000 + 100 + 18 Ⓒ 4000 + 100 + 10 + 8
Ⓑ 4000 + 10 + 8   Ⓓ 4000 + 1 + 8

ANSWER
The correct answer is
B 4000 + 10 + 8.

NOW TRY THESE

1. Which of these has a four in the ten thousands place?
   Ⓐ 367,523   Ⓒ 2,354,972
   Ⓑ 46,578   Ⓓ 4,724

2. Which of these is an odd number?
   Ⓐ 619   Ⓒ 812
   Ⓑ 400   Ⓓ 654

3. How would you write the standard form of six thousand, seven hundred thirty-six?
   Ⓐ 6,70036   Ⓒ 60,736
   Ⓑ 6,367   Ⓓ 6,736

4. Which number is greater than all the others?
   Ⓐ 9,999   Ⓒ 16,789
   Ⓑ 16,780   Ⓓ 6,799

5. In the number 40,625, in which place is the underlined digit?
   Ⓐ ten thousands Ⓒ thousands
   Ⓑ hundreds   Ⓓ tens

6. In the number 435,562, what number does the underlined digit name?
   Ⓐ 500   Ⓒ 50
   Ⓑ 5,000   Ⓓ 50,000

7. In which number does the 5 have the greater place value?
   Ⓐ 5,362   Ⓒ 3,529
   Ⓑ 53,346   Ⓓ 48,258

8. What is the least number you can write using the digits 3, 2, 1, 8 ?
   Ⓐ 2,138   Ⓒ 1,238
   Ⓑ 3,218   Ⓓ 1,382

9. Which is a true sentence?
   Ⓐ 6,238 > 6,823   Ⓒ 9,321 < 10,124
   Ⓑ 4,801 > 4,892   Ⓓ 962 < 729

10. Which is the standard number for CCCLXV?
    Ⓐ 3, 065   Ⓒ 3,065
    Ⓑ 30,560   Ⓓ 365

GO ON TO NEXT PAGE ▶

© Steck-Vaughn Company   74   Test Taking 6, SV 6774-3

Name_____ Date _____

Unit Seven: Math Concepts and Computation

Part two

DIRECTIONS ▶ Darken the circle for the correct answer. Darken the circle for Not given if the correct answer is not shown.

STRATEGY TIPS

1. Do the first step in computation, then check each answer choice.
2. Cross out the choices that are wrong.
3. When multiplying two-digit numbers, line up digits correctly.

Sample:

```
    46        Ⓐ  1,242
  x 27        Ⓑ  824
              Ⓒ  1,224
              Ⓓ  Not given
```

ANSWER
The correct answer is
A 1,242.

NOW TRY THESE

11.   67   Ⓐ 39
      + __   Ⓑ 35
      92   Ⓒ 25
                Ⓓ Not given

12. 34)̄73,916   Ⓐ 2,174
                        Ⓑ 6,234
                        Ⓒ 2,674
                        Ⓓ Not given

13.   4,780   Ⓐ 12,783
      5,791   Ⓑ 102,833
        208   Ⓒ 13,833
    + 3,054   Ⓓ Not given

14.   7,756   Ⓐ 3,126
    – 4,610   Ⓑ 3,246
                     Ⓒ 3,266
                     Ⓓ Not given

15.   5,789   Ⓐ 3,413,813
    x 607   Ⓑ 3,513,923
                   Ⓒ 3,502,923
                   Ⓓ Not given

16. 32)̄9400   Ⓐ 294
                   Ⓑ 293 r 21
                   Ⓒ 293 r 26
                   Ⓓ Not given

17.   4,672   Ⓐ 8,380
    + 3,708   Ⓑ 8,370
                     Ⓒ 7,380
                     Ⓓ Not given

18.   619,724   Ⓐ 641,173
    + 21,449   Ⓑ 630,163
                     Ⓒ 640,173
                     Ⓓ Not given

19.   83,019   Ⓐ 11,189
    – 71,821   Ⓑ 11,098
                    Ⓒ 12,198
                    Ⓓ Not given

20. ___ – 38 = 91   Ⓐ 139
                         Ⓑ 129
                         Ⓒ 120
                         Ⓓ Not given

STOP

Your time:_____

Number right:_____

Name_____ Date _____

Lesson 2: Understanding number theory and using estimation

Part one

 Darken the circle for the correct answer. Darken the circle for Not given if the correct answer is not shown.

STRATEGY TIPS

1. Use scratch paper to work each problem.
2. Try each answer choice in the problem, then choose your answer.

Sample:
What number would make this sentence true?

(4 + 4) + 3 = (5 + ___) + 2

- Ⓐ 0
- Ⓑ 3
- Ⓒ 4
- Ⓓ Not given

The correct answer is *C 4*.

NOW TRY THESE

1. Which number correctly completes this number sentence?

   (5 + 3) + 14 = 3 + (__ + 14)

   - Ⓐ 6
   - Ⓑ 5
   - Ⓒ 9
   - Ⓓ Not given

2. Which are factors of 12?
   - Ⓐ 11,1
   - Ⓑ 3,4
   - Ⓒ 10,2
   - Ⓓ Not given

3. Which are prime factors of 18?
   - Ⓐ 2 x 9
   - Ⓑ 6 x 3
   - Ⓒ 2 x 3 x 3
   - Ⓓ Not given

4. Which sentence shows 24 as a product of prime factors?
   - Ⓐ 2 x 3 x 4
   - Ⓑ 2 x 3 x 2 x 2
   - Ⓒ 12 x 2
   - Ⓓ Not given

Part two

5. The closest estimate of 42 x 28 is ___.
   - Ⓐ 2200
   - Ⓑ 1400
   - Ⓒ 1200
   - Ⓓ Not given

6. The closest estimate of $18.15 – $3.27 is ___.
   - Ⓐ $14
   - Ⓑ $15
   - Ⓒ $16
   - Ⓓ Not given

7. The closest estimate of 1800 ÷ 800 is between ____.
   - Ⓐ 4 and 5
   - Ⓑ 2 and 3
   - Ⓒ 1 and 2
   - Ⓓ Not given

8. Two books cost $5.98 together. One of the books cost $1.89. What is the closest estimate of the cost of the other book?
   - Ⓐ $3
   - Ⓑ $2
   - Ⓒ $4
   - Ⓓ Not given

Your time:_____ Number right:_____

Unit Seven: Math Concepts and Computation

Name_____   Date_____

Lesson 3: Working with fractions

DIRECTIONS ▸ Darken the circle for the correct answer.

STRATEGY TIPS

1. Remember to divide both terms of a fraction by the greatest common factor to find the simplest form of the fraction.
2. Remember that a multiple is a number that is divisible by another.

Sample:
What is the least common denominator for this set of fractions?

$$\frac{1}{3} \qquad \frac{3}{4}$$

Ⓐ 4   Ⓒ 3
Ⓑ 12 Ⓓ 7

ANSWER

The correct answer is *B 12*. *12* is the least common denominator of *3* and *4*.

NOW TRY THESE

1. What is the least common denominator for this set of fractions?

   $$\frac{7}{10} \qquad \frac{2}{3}$$

   Ⓐ 30   Ⓒ 3
   Ⓑ 10   Ⓓ 13

2. What is the simplest form for $\frac{15}{30}$?

   Ⓐ $\frac{1}{2}$ Ⓒ $\frac{5}{10}$
   Ⓑ $\frac{3}{6}$ Ⓓ $\frac{5}{610}$

3. Which of these sentences is true?

   Ⓐ $\frac{9}{12} < \frac{8}{12}$ Ⓒ $\frac{7}{10} = \frac{21}{30}$
   Ⓑ $\frac{25}{60} > \frac{36}{60}$ Ⓓ $\frac{4}{15} = \frac{12}{30}$

4. Which is the simplest fraction that represents the shaded part of the circle?

   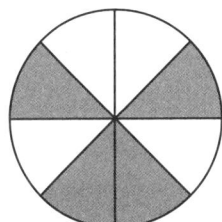

   Ⓐ $\frac{4}{8}$ Ⓒ $\frac{3}{8}$
   Ⓑ $\frac{1}{2}$ Ⓓ $\frac{2}{8}$

5. Which mixed number equals the improper fraction $\frac{20}{7}$?

   Ⓐ $3\frac{1}{7}$ Ⓒ $4\frac{1}{7}$
   Ⓑ $2\frac{5}{7}$ Ⓓ $2\frac{6}{7}$

STOP

Your time:_____

Number right:_____

Unit Seven: Math Concepts and Computation

Name_____ Date _____

Lesson 4: Working with decimals

DIRECTIONS ▶ Darken the circle for the correct answer.

STRATEGY TIPS

1. Remember that a digit in a decimal gets its value from where it is placed in relation to the decimal point.
2. In a decimal, the decimal point is written between the ones place and the tenths place.

Sample:
Which is the greatest decimal number?
Ⓐ 0.1
Ⓑ 0.205
Ⓒ 0.28
Ⓓ 0.135

ANSWER

The correct answer is C 0.28. Two tenths and 8 hundredths is greater than any of the other numbers.

NOW TRY THESE

1. What is the place value of the 7 in this number? 8.007
   Ⓐ ones
   Ⓑ tens
   Ⓒ hundredths
   Ⓓ thousandths

2. What is the standard way to write three and one hundred thirty-four thousandths?
   Ⓐ 3.034
   Ⓑ 3.304
   Ⓒ 3.134
   Ⓓ 3.0034

3. Which number sentence is true?
   Ⓐ 0.24 > 0.136
   Ⓑ 0.56 > 0.89
   Ⓒ 0.37 > 0.73
   Ⓓ $0.52 < $.46

4. 2.95
   + 0.33

   Ⓐ 2.28
   Ⓑ 3.18
   Ⓒ 3.28
   Ⓓ 2.028

5. 3.607
   + 1.568

   Ⓐ 5.175
   Ⓑ 4.175
   Ⓒ 5.205
   Ⓓ 4.165

6. $3.40 − $1.56 =
   Ⓐ $0.84
   Ⓑ $1.84
   Ⓒ $1.16
   Ⓓ $2.06

7. 0.68
   × 0.4

   Ⓐ 2.72
   Ⓑ 0.270
   Ⓒ 0.272
   Ⓓ 2.072

STOP

Your time:_____

Number right:_____

Name_____ Date_____

Lesson 5: Working with ratio, percent, and probability

DIRECTIONS ▶ Darken the circle for the correct answer. Darken the circle for Not given if the correct answer is not shown.

STRATEGY TIPS
1. Remember that ratio is a way of comparing numbers.
2. When a number is part of 100, the ratio is called a percent.

Sample:
Which fraction expresses the ratio of 26 students to 1 teacher?

Ⓐ $\frac{1}{26}$ Ⓒ $\frac{26}{1}$

Ⓑ $\frac{26}{26}$ Ⓓ Not given

ANSWER
The correct answer is C $\frac{26}{1}$. This ratio compares the number of students (26) to the number of teachers (1).

NOW TRY THESE

1. Change $\frac{9}{25}$ to a percent.
   Ⓐ 25%   Ⓒ 36%
   Ⓑ 9%   Ⓓ Not given

2. Change $\frac{4}{9}$ to a percent.
   Ⓐ 40%   Ⓒ 45%
   Ⓑ 44.4%   Ⓓ Not given

DIRECTIONS ▶ Use the circle graph to answer questions 3-5.

There are 520 students at Central Middle School. This graph shows the number of students who own pets and the kind of pets they own.

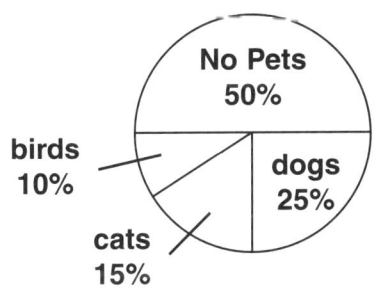

3. How many students do not own pets?
   Ⓐ 520   Ⓒ 320
   Ⓑ 260   Ⓓ Not given

4. How many students own dogs?
   Ⓐ 150   Ⓒ 130
   Ⓑ 160   Ⓓ Not given

5. How many students own cats?
   Ⓐ 90   Ⓒ 60
   Ⓑ 72   Ⓓ Not given

Your time:_____
Number right:_____

Name _____   Date _____

Lesson 6: Understanding geometry and measurement

DIRECTIONS ▶ Darken the circle for the correct answer.

STRATEGY TIPS

1. Use the objects shown or named to help you answer the questions.
2. Look for key words such as *perimeter* and *area*.

Sample:

What is the area of this figure in square units?

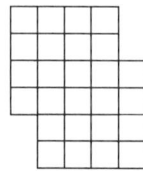

Ⓐ 32 square units
Ⓑ 21 square units
Ⓒ 26 square units
Ⓓ 24 square units

ANSWER

The correct answer is *C 26 square units*. Count the number of square units to find the area.

NOW TRY THESE

1. Which shapes are congruent?

   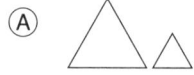   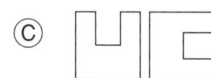

2. How many angles are in this figure?

   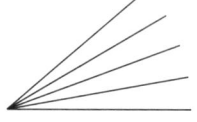

   Ⓐ 4 angles   Ⓒ 5 angles
   Ⓑ 10 angles   Ⓓ 1 angle

3. Which angle is an acute angle?

   Ⓐ    Ⓒ

   Ⓑ   Ⓓ

4. What is the perimeter of this garden plot?

   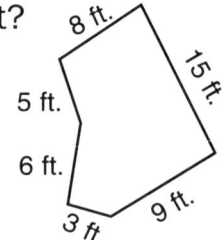

   Ⓐ 46 feet   Ⓒ 21 feet
   Ⓑ 24 feet   Ⓓ 23 feet

5. Which figure has four congruent sides?

   Ⓐ parallelogram   Ⓒ pentagon
   Ⓑ rectangle   Ⓓ square

GO ON TO NEXT PAGE

Name _____   Date _____

Unit VII, lesson 6, page 2

6. Which of the following is a line segment in this figure?

   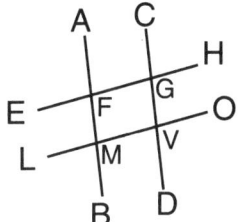

   Ⓐ $\overline{BD}$ Ⓑ $\overline{GH}$ Ⓒ $\overline{AC}$ Ⓓ $\overline{EL}$

7. What is the area of a classroom that is 24 feet by 19 feet?

   Ⓐ 456 ft²   Ⓒ 240 ft²
   Ⓑ 624 ft²   Ⓓ 190 ft²

8. Which units of measurement are used to measure the weight of meat?

   Ⓐ liters   Ⓒ grams
   Ⓑ degrees   Ⓓ meters

9. Which is used to measure liquid capacity?

   Ⓐ grams   Ⓒ pounds
   Ⓑ meters   Ⓓ liters

10. What is the volume of this cube?

    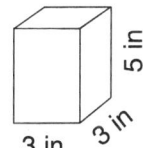

    Ⓐ 11 cubic inches
    Ⓑ 45 cubic inches
    Ⓒ 30 cubic inches
    Ⓓ 40 cubic inches

11. $\frac{3}{4}$ pound = ____ ounces?

    Ⓐ 16 ounces   Ⓒ 12 ounces
    Ⓑ 8 ounces   Ⓓ 4 ounces

12. The length of a pencil would best be measured in _____.

    Ⓐ feet   Ⓒ inches
    Ⓑ yards   Ⓓ miles

13. The height of a building is best expressed in _____.

    Ⓐ meters   Ⓒ liters
    Ⓑ grams   Ⓓ degrees

14. Which pair of lines is parallel?

    Ⓐ 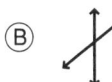   Ⓒ

    Ⓑ   Ⓓ

STOP

Your time: _____
Number right: _____

On this lesson I did _____ because _____

_____.

I think it would help me to _____

_____.

Name_____ Date_____

Lesson 7: Using graphs and tables

DIRECTIONS ▶ Darken the circle for the correct answer.

STRATEGY TIPS
1. Study the graph key carefully.
2. As you read the question, look for the words and numbers.

Sample:
This graph shows the number of stuffed animals four girls own.

Which girl has more than 9 but fewer than 14?

Ⓐ Maggie   Ⓒ Julie
Ⓑ Kyra   Ⓓ Ashley

Answer: The correct answer is *B Kyra*. Each picture is equal to 3 stuffed animals. Kyra has twelve.

NOW TRY THESE

This graph shows the amount of different snack foods Quinn sold when he worked at the movie theater. Study the graph. Then answer questions 1-4.

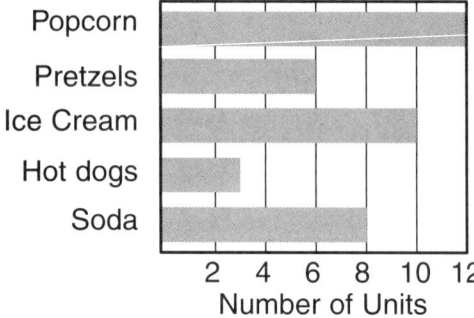

1. Which are the most popular snacks?
   Ⓐ hot dogs and soda
   Ⓑ popcorn and pretzels
   Ⓒ popcorn and ice cream
   Ⓓ pretzels and ice cream

2. How many ice cream bars did Quinn sell?
   Ⓐ 6   Ⓒ 11
   Ⓑ 4   Ⓓ 10

3. How many units of soda and pretzels were sold altogether?
   Ⓐ 14 units   Ⓒ 6 units
   Ⓑ 8 units   Ⓓ 10 units

4. Which question cannot be answered by studying the graph?
   Ⓐ How many snacks were sold altogether?
   Ⓑ How many people bought more than one snack?
   Ⓒ Which is the least popular snack?
   Ⓓ How many more units of ice cream than soda were sold?

Your time:_____   Number right:_____

Test Seven: Math Concepts and Computation

Name_____ Date _____

PRACTICE TEST 7
Part 1

Directions: For questions 1-9, darken the circle on the answer sheet for the correct answer.

Sample:
Which is the expanded form of 6,007?

- A six hundred seven
- B six thousand seven hundred
- C six thousand seven
- D six thousand seventy

Answer: The correct answer is *C six thousand seven.*

---

1. Which group of numbers goes from the least to the greatest?

   - A 653;356;536
   - B 241;421;124
   - C 197;719;917
   - D 137;731;317

2. What is the value of the underlined digit?   78<u>3</u>,495

   - A thousands
   - B hundred thousands
   - C tens
   - D ten thousands

3. Which is a true sentence?

   - A 8,057 > 8,507
   - B 1,216 < 1,261
   - C 7,235 > 7,325
   - D 9,180 < 9,081

4.   8,010
     − 3,762

   - A 4,248
   - B 5,358
   - C 7,900
   - D 4,342

5. Round the numbers to the nearest thousand. Then add.

      8,954
    +1,853

   - A 10,000
   - B 7,000
   - C 10,500
   - D 11,000

6. Name 100 more than 945.

   - A 955
   - B 1,945
   - C 1,045
   - D 1,145

7.   6,416
    x 370

   - A 2,373,920
   - B 2,383,920
   - C 1,373,820
   - D 1,963,820

8. 705 r8 = ? ÷ 32

   - A 21,568
   - B 22,568
   - C 21,570
   - D 22,658

9. Which is <u>not</u> a factor of 4?

   - A 2
   - B 4
   - C 1
   - D 6

83

Test Seven: Math Concepts and Computation

Name_____ Date _____

Part 2

Directions: For questions 10-15, darken the circle on the answer sheet for the correct answer. Darken *E Not given* if the correct answer is not shown.

Sample:
Which is the simplest answer?

$3\frac{9}{21}$
$-2\frac{2}{21}$

A $1\frac{7}{21}$
B $1\frac{1}{3}$
C $1\frac{5}{21}$
D $2\frac{1}{3}$
E Not given

Answer: The correct answer is *B* $1\frac{1}{3}$.

---

10. Which is the simplest fraction that represents the shaded part of the rectangle?

    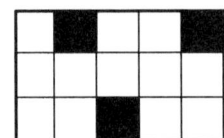

    A $\frac{3}{15}$
    B $\frac{9}{15}$
    C $\frac{1}{5}$
    D $\frac{3}{5}$
    E Not given

11. Which mixed number represents the improper fraction?

    $\frac{19}{4}$

    A $4\frac{3}{4}$
    B $15\frac{1}{4}$
    C $5\frac{3}{4}$
    D $12\frac{1}{4}$
    E Not given

12. Which is the least common denominator for these mixed numbers?

    $3\frac{5}{6}$, $7\frac{3}{8}$

    A 16
    B 24
    C 18
    D 48
    E Not given

13. Estimate the difference to the nearest dollar.
    $2.14 – $0.71

    A $1.50
    B $2.00
    C $1.00
    D $1.45
    E Not given

14. $32\overline{)20.864}$

    A 29
    B 2.8
    C 2.08
    D .28
    E Not given

15. Four and three hundred three thousandths is written _____.

    A 4.330
    B 4.030
    C 4.303
    D 43.30
    E Not given

GO ON TO NEXT PAGE

Name_____ Date _____

Test Seven: Math Concepts and Computation

Part 3

Study the diagram. Then answer questions 16 and 17.

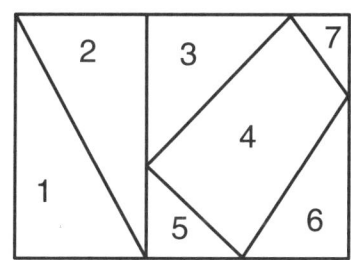

16. Which two figures are congruent shapes?

    A 1 and 4   C 3 and 4
    B 2 and 5   D 1 and 2

17. How many triangles can be found in the diagram?

    A 2   C 6
    B 5   D 4

18. Which word describes these lines?

    A parallel   C intersecting
    B segments   D perpendicular

19. What is the area of a square that is 5m by 7m?

    A 12m   C 24m
    B 35m   D 40m

20. What time will it be in 35 minutes?

    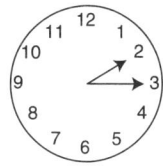

    A 2:35   C 2:50
    B 3:15   D 3:05

Study the line graph of the hours per week that Kim watches TV. Then answer questions 21 and 22.

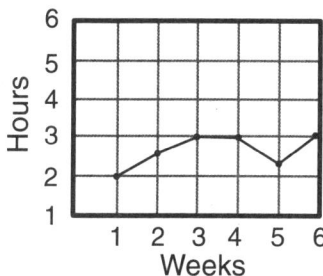

Kim's TV Watching

21. How many hours did Kim watch TV during week 2?

    A $3\frac{1}{2}$ hours   C 2 hours
    B $2\frac{1}{2}$ hours   D 1 hour

22. In which weeks did Kim watch 3 hours of TV?

    A 1,3,5   C 3,4,6
    B 2,3,6   D 2,3,4

Suggested Time Limit: 25 minutes   Your time: _____
Check your work if you have time. Wait for instructions from your teacher.

Name_____   Date_____

UNIT VIII: PROBLEM SOLVING

Lesson 1: Understanding problem solving strategies

DIRECTIONS ▶ Darken the circle for the correct strategy to use.

STRATEGY TIPS
1. Read each problem carefully.
2. Make a mental picture.
3. What are you asked to find out?
4. What information is given?

Sample:

Amber and Wayne went blueberry picking last week. For every 3 pints that Amber picked, Wayne picked 4. Together they picked 35 pints. How many pints did Amber pick?

Ⓐ Make a list   Ⓒ Count backwards
Ⓑ Make a table   Ⓓ Guess and check

ANSWER
The correct answer is B *Make a table.* The table will show you the ratio of pints Amber picked compared to the pints that Wayne picked.

NOW TRY THESE

1. Northside School is holding an election next week. There are 8 classrooms in the school. Each class has 32 students. If all the students are present, how many votes will be cast?

   Ⓐ Find the pattern   Ⓒ Choose an operation
   Ⓑ Guess and check   Ⓓ Use estimation

2. Mr. Germaine set out 350 tomato seedlings. If every plant yields about 15 tomatoes, about how many tomatoes can he expect to harvest?

   Ⓐ Make a list   Ⓒ Make a graph
   Ⓑ Use estimation   Ⓓ Count backwards

3. The Brady family is buying new carpet for their living room. The room is 14 feet long and 12 feet wide. Carpet World delivered 187 square feet of carpet. How many square feet are not needed?

   Ⓐ More than one step   Ⓒ Identify extra information
   Ⓑ Work backwards   Ⓓ Use a table

GO ON TO NEXT PAGE

Name _____   Date _____

Unit VIII, lesson 1, page 2

4. A reporter wrote a story about a fire downtown. His story had 420 words. He worked on the story for three hours. Then he added 52 more words. How many words were in the story?

    Ⓐ Too little information   Ⓒ Identify extra information
    Ⓑ More than one step   Ⓓ Guess and check

5. Perry collects baseball cards. If you divide the number of cards he has by 2 and add 74 the result is 129. How many cards does Perry have?

    Ⓐ Choose an operation   Ⓒ Use estimation
    Ⓑ Make a table   Ⓓ Work backwards

6. Chelsea lives the farthest from school. Lucia lives between Gina and Tony. Paige lives nearer to school than Tony. Who lives between Paige and Gina?

    Ⓐ Guess and check   Ⓒ Make a drawing
    Ⓑ Choose an operation   Ⓓ Estimate

7. Ramon is making posters for the school play. He has a purple marker, a brown marker, a red marker, and a green marker. He also has blue poster paper and white poster paper. If he uses only one color marker for each poster, how many different kinds of posters can he make?

    Ⓐ Identify extra information   Ⓒ Make a drawing
    Ⓑ Choose an operation   Ⓓ Work backwards

8. The rules for soccer playoffs this year say each team is allowed to play another team only once. If there are two teams, 1 game will be played. Three teams will play 3 games. Four teams will play 6 games. How many games will five teams play?

    Ⓐ Guess and check   Ⓒ Choose an operation
    Ⓑ Find a pattern   Ⓓ Use estimation

STOP

Your time: _____

Number right: _____

On this lesson I did _____ because _____

_____.

I think it would help me to _____

_____.

Name_____   Date _____

Lesson 2: Practicing problem solving

DIRECTIONS ▶ Darken the circle for the correct answer to each problem. Darken *D not enough information* if you think you need more information to solve the problem.

STRATEGY TIPS

1. Read the problem carefully.
2. What facts are given?
3. What is the question?
4. Decide on a strategy to use.

Sample:

Sandy is making clothespin dolls to sell at a craft show. She makes 1 doll the first day, 5 the second day, 9 the third day, and so on. How many dolls will Sandy have after 5 days?

Ⓐ 13 dolls   Ⓒ 45 dolls
Ⓑ 17 dolls   Ⓓ not enough information

ANSWER

The correct answer is *C 45 dolls*. The pattern shows that Sandy makes 4 more dolls each day than she did the day before, so in 5 days she will have made 45 dolls.

NOW TRY THESE

1. Eve is making a new sweater to wear with her jeans. She found some buttons that she wanted to use. There were 4 buttons on a card. How many cards of buttons will she need?

   Ⓐ 4 cards   Ⓒ 3 cards
   Ⓑ 1 card   Ⓓ not enough information

2. Dr. Fine's office hours are 9:15 A.M. to 11:45 A.M. and again from 2:15 P.M. to 6:30 P.M. How much time does she spend in the office each day?

   Ⓐ 5 hours and 30 minutes   Ⓒ 6 hours and 45 minutes
   Ⓑ 6 hours   Ⓓ not enough information

3. In the last election, 2,485 people in District 21 voted for governor; 1,782 were women. In District 45, 2,097 people voted for governor; 924 people voted early in the morning. How many more people voted in district 21 than in District 45?

   Ⓐ 388   Ⓒ 1173
   Ⓑ 1159   Ⓓ not enough information

Name _____   Date _____

Unit VIII, lesson 2, page 2

Ms. Davis' class organized a recycling project. They collected paper, cans, and glass and brought them to the recycling center. The drive lasted four weeks. Use the table below to answer questions 4-10.

	Paper	Glass	Cans
Week 1	125 lbs.	62 lbs.	55 lbs.
Week 2	178 lbs.	75 lbs.	49 lbs.
Week 3	202 lbs.	48 lbs.	42 lbs.
Week 4	183 lbs.	80 lbs.	61 lbs.

4. How many pounds of paper were collected during the last two weeks of the drive?
   - Ⓐ 313 pounds
   - Ⓒ 380 pounds
   - Ⓑ 385 pounds
   - Ⓓ 320 pounds

5. How many pounds of glass were collected altogether?
   - Ⓐ 104 pounds
   - Ⓒ 265 pounds
   - Ⓑ 103 pounds
   - Ⓓ 189 pounds

6. How many pounds of material were collected during the second week?
   - Ⓐ 178 pounds
   - Ⓒ 49 pounds
   - Ⓑ 75 pounds
   - Ⓓ 302 pounds

7. How many more pounds of paper were collected during the fourth week than the first week?
   - Ⓐ 58 pounds
   - Ⓒ 55 pounds
   - Ⓑ 19 pounds
   - Ⓓ 32 pounds

8. A recycling company pays $0.40 for each pound of aluminum. How much money did the class earn for the aluminum cans at the end of the drive?
   - Ⓐ $120.00
   - Ⓒ $160.00
   - Ⓑ $182.40
   - Ⓓ $82.80

9. The class earned $26.50 for the glass they collected. How much did they earn per pound?
   - Ⓐ $0.20 per pound
   - Ⓒ $0.10 per pound
   - Ⓑ $0.70 per pound
   - Ⓓ not enough information

10. If the class earned $172.00 for the paper, how much did they earn altogether for the paper, the cans, and the glass?
    - Ⓐ $310.70
    - Ⓒ $308.58
    - Ⓑ $281.30
    - Ⓓ not enough information

Name_____ Date _____

Unit VIII, lesson 2, page 3

Study this diagram. Then answer question 11.

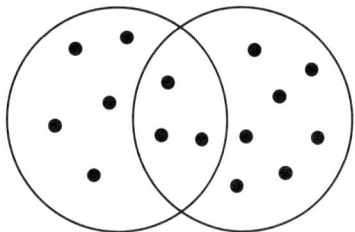

11. Theresa's class is going on an outing. Eight students want to go hiking. Ten students want to go swimming. Three students would like to do both activities. How many students want to do at least one of the activities?

    Ⓐ eight students Ⓒ fifteen students
    Ⓑ ten students   Ⓓ three students

12. Rudy likes to build model planes. He bought two new kits for $25.98 and a display stand for $7.95. How much more did he spend for the kits than the display stand?

    Ⓐ $33.93   Ⓒ $17.03
    Ⓑ $18.03   Ⓓ $8.03

13. The product of two numbers is 875. One number is 10 more than the other number. What are the two numbers?

    Ⓐ 35 and 20   Ⓒ 25 and 35
    Ⓑ 25 and 45   Ⓓ not enough information

14. Keiyo is in charge of setting up chairs on the lawn for the school carnival. She plans to have 28 rows with 12 chairs in each row. About how many seats will there be?

    Ⓐ about 280 seats   Ⓒ about 300 seats
    Ⓑ about 320 seats   Ⓓ about 310 seats

STOP

Your time: _____

Number right: _____

On this lesson I did _____ because _____

_____.

I think it would help me to _____

_____.

Name _____ Date _____

PRACTICE TEST 8

Part 1

Directions: For questions 1-6, darken the circle for the answer that tells what strategy to use in order to solve the problem. Record your answer on the answer sheet.

Sample:

Alex is practicing to try out for the swim team. He did 2 laps the first day, 5 the second day, 8 the third day, and 11 the fourth day. How many laps will he do on the sixth day?

A Guess and check
B Use estimation
C Find a pattern
D Work backwards

Answer: The correct answer is *C Find a pattern.*

---

1. Keisha has 9 coins. Their total value is $0.83. What coins and how many of each does she have?

   A Choose an operation
   B Guess and check
   C Make a graph
   D Too little information

2. The Alwyn family is planning to rent bicycles when they go on vacation. Each bike costs $8 a day to rent. How much will the family have to spend for the bicycles?

   A Use a table
   B Identify extra information
   C Too little information
   D Guess and check

3. Sharon had $86 at the end of the first day of the craft fair. She made $38 in the morning. The rent for the booth was $15. How much money did she start out with?

   A Make a graph
   B Find a pattern
   C Work backwards
   D Make a list

4. Suki works as a baby sitter five hours a week. She earns $3.50 an hour. Her friend Carol earns $3.85 an hour. How much money does Suki earn in two weeks?

   A Use estimation
   B Make a table
   C Guess and check
   D Identify extra information

Name_____ Date_____

Practice test 8, part 1, page 2

5. Olga bought 9 packages of seeds for her garden. Each package contains 25 seeds. How many seeds will Olga be planting?

   A Choose an operation   C Make a table
   B Work backwards   D Find a pattern

6. The Wheatly School ordered 28 new bookcases for some of its classrooms. If they put 4 bookcases in each classroom, how many rooms will get new bookcases?

   A Work backwards   C Choose an operation
   B Identify extra information D Guess and check

Part 2

Directions: For questions 7-19, darken the circle for the correct answer. Record your answers on the answer sheet.

Sample:
   Sophie bought a cookie for $0.59 and a container of milk for $0.44. About how much money did she spend?

   A $1.00   C $1.10
   B $0.90   D $1.20

   Answer: The correct answer is *A $1.00.*

7. Sara walked her neighbor's dog 2 times in September and 3 times in October. She was paid $5 each time she walked the dog. How much money did Sara earn altogether?

   A $30   C $20
   B $25   D $15

This graph shows the number and kinds of books a chain of bookstores sold in one month. Study the graph and then use it to answer questions 8-10.

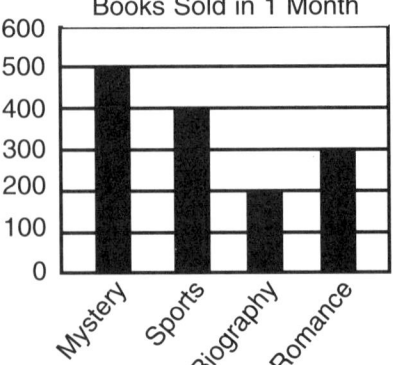

8. How many mystery books were sold?

   A 600   C 300
   B 400   D 500

GO ON TO NEXT PAGE

Name _____   Date _____

Practice test 8, part 2, page 2

9. How many more sports books than romance novels were sold?

   A 200   C 100
   B 300   D 400

10. How many books were sold altogether?

    A 1,500   C 14,000
    B 1,400   D 12,000

11. In 1990 there were 1,236 students at Madison High School. What else do you need to know to find out the percent of increase in students in 1997?

    A The number of students who graduated.
    B The number of students who moved.
    C The number of students enrolled in 1997.
    D The number of teachers.

12. There are 12 classes at Meadow Drive Middle School. Each class has one 50–minute music period per week. Which number sentence would you use to find out how much time the music teacher spends with all of the classes each week?

    A 12 x 50 = __   C 12 + __ = 50
    B 50 ÷ __ = 12   D __ − 50 = 12

13. The new multiplex cinemas use giant screens in all their theaters. Each screen is 138 feet wide and 42 feet high. About how many square feet is the area of each screen?

    A about 5,000   C about 6,000
    B about 9,000   D about 4,000

Name_____ Date _____

Practice test 8, part 2, page 3

Liza saved $150 to take special dance classes. The circle graph shows what percent of her money was spent in different ways. Study the graph carefully and then answer questions 14-18.

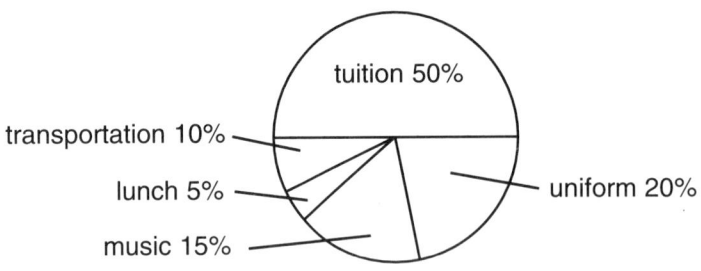

14. How much did Liza spend for tuition?

    A $50   C $25
    B $75   D $30

15. How much did she spend for music?

    A $15   C $15.50
    B $10   D $22.50

16. On which item does Liza spend the least amount of money?

    A transportation   C tuition
    B lunch   D uniform

17. What percent of her money is spent on tuition and music combined?

    A 50%   C 65%
    B 15%   D 35%

18. What percent of her money is spent on transportation, lunch, and uniforms?

    A 5%   C 90%
    B 35%   D 50%

19. Maria has to pack her mother's antique Christmas ornaments in special boxes. Each box has eight compartments. How many boxes does Maria need to pack 54 ornaments?

    A 9   C 10
    B 7   D 8

Suggested Time Limit: 28 minutes   Your time: _____
Check your work if you have time. Wait for instructions from your teacher.

TEST TAKING: GRADE 6
ANSWER KEY

UNIT ONE
LESSON 1 pp. 7-8
1. C
2. B
3. D
4. B
5. C
6. A
7. A
8. C
9. B
10. D
11. C

LESSON 2 p. 9
1. D
2. B
3. D
4. B
5. D
6. A
7. B
8. A
9. C
10. C

LESSON 3 pp. 10-11
1. A
2. C
3. A
4. D
5. B
6. A
7. C
8. A
9. B
10. B
11. D

LESSON 4 p. 12
1. C
2. B
3. A
4. C
5. D
6. C
7. B
8. C

TEST ONE pp. 13-15
1. B
2. A
3. B
4. C
5. C
6. A
7. A
8. C
9. A
10. C
11. B
12. C
13. A
14. B
15. D
16. A
17. C
18. B
19. A

UNIT TWO
LESSON 1 pp. 16-17
1. A
2. C
3. B
4. E
5. B
6. A
7. B
8. B
9. A
10. C
11. A
12. D
13. A
14. A
15. B
16. C

LESSON 2 p. 18
1. C
2. A
3. B
4. A
5. C
6. B
7. E
8. B

LESSON 3 pp. 19-20
1. A
2. C
3. A
4. B
5. C
6. D
7. D
8. C
9. A
10. D
11. E
12. C
13. B

LESSON 4 p. 21
1. D
2. B
3. D
4. A
5. D
6. C

LESSON 5 pp. 22-23
1. C
2. B
3. B
4. C
5. C
6. A
7. B
8. C
9. A
10. C
11. D
12. B

TEST TWO pp. 24-27
1. A
2. B
3. D
4. A
5. D
6. B
7. A
8. B
9. C
10. E
11. B
12. C
13. A
14. C
15. B
16. A
17. C
18. B
19. B
20. D
21. B
22. D

UNIT THREE
LESSON 1 p. 28
1. B
2. A
3. B
4. C
5. A

LESSON 2 p. 29
1. B
2. D
3. C
4. B
5. C
6. B

LESSON 3 p. 30
1. D
2. C
3. A
4. D
5. C
6. D

LESSON 4 p. 31
1. A
2. C
3. B
4. D
5. D
6. A
7. A
8. B
9. C
10. C

TEST THREE pp. 32-34
1. A
2. B
3. C
4. D
5. C
6. D
7. A
8. C
9. D
10. B
11. C
12. B
13. A
14. C
15. D
16. A
17. A
18. D
19. B
20. C

UNIT FOUR
LESSON 1 p. 35
1. C
2. B
3. B
4. D
5. C
6. D
7. A
8. C

LESSON 2 p. 36
1. C
2. E
3. A
4. C
5. E

LESSON 3 pp. 37-38
1. B
2. C
3. A
4. A
5. B
6. D
7. B
8. A
9. C
10. B

LESSON 4 p. 39
1. B
2. A
3. C
4. B
5. D

LESSON 5 pp. 40-41
1. C
2. B
3. A
4. C
5. E
6. B
7. C
8. E
9. B
10. B
11. B
12. C
13. B
14. B
15. B
16. C

LESSON 6 pp. 42-43
1. D
2. A
3. C
4. A
5. D
6. B
7. B
8. D
9. B
10. D
11. A
12. C
13. B
14. A
15. B

LESSON 7 p. 44
1. D
2. B
3. A
4. B
5. C
6. D

TEST TAKING: GRADE 6
ANSWER KEY

TEST FOUR
pp. 45-49
1. B
2. D
3. A
4. B
5. D
6. C
7. A
8. B
9. D
10. A
11. E
12. D
13. E
14. A
15. C
16. C
17. D
18. B
19. B
20. B
21. B
22. A
23. A
24. B
25. B
26. A
27. C
28. C
29. B
30. C
31. B

UNIT FIVE
LESSON 1 pp. 50-51
1. B
2. C
3. D
4. A
5. B
6. C
7. D

LESSON 2 pp. 52-53
1. A
2. D
3. B
4. D
5. B
6. C
7. B
8. C

LESSON 3 p. 54
1. D
2. C
3. B
4. B
5. A
6. B

LESSON 4 p. 55
1. C
2. B
3. C
4. A

LESSON 5 pp. 56-57
1. B
2. A
3. D
4. B
5. B
6. A
7. B
8. B
9. B
10. B

TEST FIVE pp. 58-61
1. B
2. C
3. A
4. B
5. B
6. A
7. D
8. C
9. C
10. D
11. A
12. C
13. C
14. A
15. C
16. C

UNIT SIX
LESSON 1 pp. 62-63
1. E
2. A
3. A
4. C

LESSON 2 pp. 64-65
1. B
2. C
3. B

LESSON 3 pp. 66-67
1. C
2. B
3. A
4. C

LESSON 4 pp. 68-69
1. D
2. B
3. A
4. C

TEST SIX pp. 70-73
1. D
2. A
3. B
4. C
5. A

UNIT SEVEN
LESSON 1 pp. 74-75
1. B
2. A
3. D
4. C
5. B
6. A
7. B
8. C
9. C
10. D
11. C
12. A
13. C
14. D
15. B
16. D
17. A
18. A
19. D
20. B

LESSON 2 p. 76
1. B
2. B
3. C
4. B
5. C
6. B
7. B
8. C

LESSON 3 p. 77
1. A
2. A
3. C
4. B
5. D

LESSON 4 p. 78
1. D
2. C
3. A
4. C
5. A
6. B
7. C

LESSON 5 p. 79
1. C
2. B
3. B
4. C
5. D

LESSON 6 pp. 80-81
1. C
2. B
3. C
4. A
5. D
6. B
7. A
8. C
9. D
10. B
11. C
12. C
13. A
14. A

LESSON 7 p. 82
1. C
2. D
3. A
4. B

TEST SEVEN pp. 83-87
1. C
2. D
3. B
4. A
5. D
6. C
7. A
8. B
9. D
10. C
11. A
12. B
13. C
14. E
15. C
16. D
17. C
18. C
19. B
20. C
21. B
22. C

UNIT EIGHT
LESSON 1 pp. 86-87
1. C
2. B
3. A
4. C
5. D
6. C
7. C
8. B

LESSON 2 pp. 88-90
1. D
2. C
3. A
4. B
5. C
6. D
7. A
8. D
9. C
10. B
11. C
12. B
13. C
14. C

TEST EIGHT pp. 91-94
1. D
2. C
3. C
4. D
5. A
6. C
7. B
8. D
9. C
10. B
11. C
12. A
13. C
14. B
15. D
16. B
17. C
18. B
19. B